Soldier Groups / and

DAVID G. MANDELBAUM

Negro Soldiers

1952
UNIVERSITY OF CALIFORNIA PRESS
BERKELEY AND LOS ANGELES

UNIVERSITY OF CALIFORNIA PRESS
BERKELEY AND LOS ANGELES, CALIFORNIA

CAMBRIDGE UNIVERSITY PRESS, LONDON, ENGLAND

COPYRIGHT, 1952, BY
THE REGENTS OF THE UNIVERSITY OF CALIFORNIA

BY THE UNIVERSITY OF CALIFORNIA PRINTING DEPARTMENT
DESIGNED BY JOHN B. GOETZ

TO MY FATHER

Contents /

Introduction /

There is a collection of
military essays called
Battle Studies which has been read assiduously by several
generations of career officers. Part of it was first published
as a pamphlet in 1868 and the rest put together from the
author's notes after he was killed by a stray projectile
from a Prussian gun during the Franco-Prussian War in
1870. The author, Colonel Ardant du Picq, stresses the
importance of morale over matériel in battle. This was a
popular doctrine among French generals before World
War I, not always to the benefit of their military fortunes,
and has again become popularly discussed, if not well
understood, among military writers more recently, when
morale seemed a vital factor.

The difficulty with such discussions, and not only those
by military men, is that the term "morale" is used in
widely differing ways and refers to concepts which are
usually elusively and vaguely formulated. Ardant du
Picq equates the soldier's morale with his discipline,

which includes "respect for and confidence in his chiefs; confidence in his comrades and fear of their reproaches and retaliation if he abandons them in danger; his desire to go where others do without trembling more than they; in a word, the whole of esprit de corps." (Ardant du Picq, p. 122.)

These comrades are still important to the soldier and influence his behavior in training and in garrison as well as in combat. Indeed, morale—however defined—frequently turns out to vary according to the soldier's relations to a group of comrades and according to the nature of social relations within such a group.

This group is usually called the "primary group" in the following pages because that term has had widest usage in the literature. "Nuclear group" is another and perhaps a better term which is applicable. Both terms denote the small, informal groupings which are important in much of human social activity. As used here in the discussion of military organization, the primary or nuclear group refers to the set of men who are close friends and who form a coöperating social nucleus in most phases of a soldier's life.

Although the men of this group are first brought together through the impersonal operation of the formal military organization, once they establish their alliance they manage to aid each other in many varied ways and to stay together through diverse situations. They not only coöperate in the manner prescribed by regulations, but also in ways which are not so prescribed or are even proscribed by official rule.

Other terms often used for this kind of intimate alliance, are "the informal group," "the face-to-face group," "the clique," "the autonomous group."

Our major interest in Part I of this survey is in the primary group, its relation to the formal structure of the army, to the "respect for and confidence in his chiefs," and to the goals of the larger organization. Few parts of Western social organization are more explicitly defined than the formal organization of a modern army and few have been less well analyzed as they actually function. Essential to an analysis of how an army unit actually operates is an understanding of the role of the primary group. For social theory, this functional analysis will help round out the general view of informal groupings within formal and relatively rigid bureaucratic organizations.

Little information is available about changes in the nature of primary groups as external conditions vary or as internal factors operate. There are probably significant differences between the primary groups of a unit guarding an airfield in North Africa and one guarding the Presidio of San Francisco, or between those in a unit of army clerks and in one of glidermen. Such differences have not yet been subject to reliable scientific observation.

But some data are available on two major differences which are considered here. One is concerned with the effect of combat on the primary group. That is discussed in the final section of Part I. The other, discussed in Part II, is concerned with the effects of grouping Negroes into all-Negro units.

The literature on Negro units contains little or no reference to the primary group. Yet the concept of the primary group is helpful in clarifying what has happened in Negro units in the U.S. armed forces and to Negroes who have fought side by side with white soldiers.

Although both parts of this survey discuss all the U.S. armed forces, the major consideration is with the Army. And the discussion of the primary group in the Army usually refers to the primary groups within an infantry rifle company. The term "unit" refers to a unit of company size except where otherwise indicated. "Outfit" refers to that unit to which the soldier has special loyalty and with which he identifies most. A soldier's outfit may be a small detachment or a battalion, depending on circumstances.

Most publications cited in the following discussion, especially of the primary group, deal with the U.S. Army as it was during World War II. There have been some changes since then, both in the military setup and in the society of which it is a part. Hence some statements may need modification, but, in the main, the analysis still holds.

The analysis has been derived from the published sources. The author's own Army service, like that of other anthropologists who have been in the services, allowed little time or opportunity for ethnological field work in the usual sense on Army culture. But most social scientists who have been in uniform will agree that while their military experience may not have permitted systematic observation, it did yield fruitful insights into military ways.

The index was prepared by Mrs. Mary Anne Whipple; the editorial assistance of Mr. Maxwell E. Knight is gratefully acknowledged.

Primary Group /

Scientific data on the primary group in the military context are extremely meager. This does not come about from any lack of interest, for it is a topic which has been considered as long as there has been interest in the reasons for military success or failure. Thus the classic *Battle Studies*, mentioned above, deals with some of the central problems formulated here. But Ardant du Picq's observations, full of insight though they are, were not systematically gathered or carefully checked. His conclusions may be interpreted in many different ways and cannot well be applied rigorously to military situations differing from those of France in the 1860's, when du Picq wrote. In short, such writings offer impressions rather than data, and belong to the field of literature rather than to that of science.

Part of the reason for the paucity of reliable data on this topic is that the concepts and techniques for the scientific investigation of the problem have been formulated relatively recently and have yet to be well developed. Hence much of the evidence relating to primary groups in the U.S. Army was gathered incidentally, as an ancillary outcome of research directed toward other problems.

This is true of the best and most comprehensive recent study of the Army, the *Studies in Social Psychology in World War II*. The four volumes of this important work are the result of the activities of the Research Branch, Information and Education Division, United States Army, during four years of World War II. The first two volumes, *The American Soldier: Adjustment during Army Life* and *The American Soldier: Combat and its Aftermath* (referred to as Stouffer, I and II) are especially useful for our purposes. An explanation of why this work is not even more useful is best given in the words of the authors.

"The problem of measuring the cooperative effort of a unit was never solved satisfactorily, and it must be set down as one of the subjects which should call for the best efforts of sociologists and psychologists in years ahead.

"Instead of solving the problem of measurement of group morale, the Research Branch, in large part, bypassed it. Faced with the necessity of giving the Army command, quickly and reliably, information which would be useful in policy making, the Research Branch concentrated primarily not on evaluation of the cooperative zeal of groups toward Army goals, but rather on study of personal adjustment. As compared with the concept of morale, it was easier to find nonverbal behavior whose relationships with the verbal behavior could be studied.

"Even though the concept of personal adjustment is an individual and not a group concept, it is nevertheless useful for group comparisons." (Stouffer, I:85.)

Not only were group dynamics difficult to observe and to measure, but the Research Branch did not find it easy to obtain the facilities necessary for the proper experimental study of key concepts in the field of group behavior. Thus the authors say:

"Even more reluctant were the authorities to permit experimental studies to test hypotheses about leadership. The social-psychological and sociological literature on this subject is filled with precepts and stereotypes which embody a great deal of common sense experience, but any substantial advance in the way of proving that if you vary X you will also vary Y depends on experimentation under controlled conditions. Not until the war neared the end was authority obtained to begin experimental studies of the effects of leadership (at the noncom level) on troop attitudes. For a few weeks a study preliminary to experimentation was carried out at an Army post in New England, but the end of the war and curtailment of research activities brought this effort to an abrupt end.

"There are few practical problems facing social science more urgent than that of studying leadership experimentally and developing some tested hypotheses to replace the copybook maxims that now fill most manuals on leadership, whether written for the Army, for industry, or for organizations like the YMCA." (Stouffer, 1:363.)

Despite these limitations, this work is the best single source of data for an understanding of the role of the primary group in the U.S. Army.

Another source of relevant information is exemplified by the papers published in *The American Journal of Sociology* for March, 1946 (vol. 51, no. 5). This issue dealt exclusively with observations on the sociology of military life. All authors of the twenty-one papers in this issue had had direct experience with human behavior under conditions of military service, most of them as officers or enlisted men. All were professionally trained in one of the social or medical sciences. These and similar studies which have appeared in other issues of this and of comparable journals, have the advantage of having been done by trained analysts who knew the data by first-hand experience. They have the disadvantage of having been written as incidental outcomes of other duties, and so were done without over-all planning, unified theoretical outlook, or cross-validation.

Some of the best source materials from the psychiatric approach are found in *Men Under Stress* by Roy R. Grinker and John P. Spiegel. The authors of this work are psychiatrists whose military duties during World War II gave them wide experience with the problems of group dynamics and also permitted systematic observation. Another work by the same authors, *War Neuroses*, and similar psychiatrically oriented studies provide some evidence on group behavior. But since the observations were made in the course of clinical work, these studies emphasize individual and abnormal cases of maladjustment rather than the normal processes of group adjustment. The data presented were mainly collected in clinics and hospitals, and only incidentally have to do with typical behavior in garrison and on the field of battle.

One work which does report battlefield behavior is *Men Against Fire* by S. L. A. Marshall. It presents the conclusions of an astute analyst from intensive and first-hand studies of leadership and unit performance in some of the major operations of World War II. Colonel Marshall's duties as a member of the Historical Division, War Department Special Staff, gave him the opportunity to make systematic observations; his knowledge of military history enabled him to view his findings in broad perspective. His book is an important document for students of military society not only for its intrinsic merit but also because of the comparative rarity of such empirical studies. Marshall puts it well in the opening note to his book:

"One of the deterrents to the adoption of new concepts

is that company officers and noncoms rarely write of their combat experiences. Even when they do so they are unlikely to search into the reason and nature of them, usually because the experiences are narrow and personal. Also, they have no way of gauging what things are typical and characteristic.

"In consequence, most of our textbooks and commentaries on leadership and the mastery of the moral problem in battle are written by senior officers who are either wholly lacking in combat experience or have been for long periods so far removed from the reality of small arms action that they have come to forget what were once their most vital convictions and impressions." (Marshall, pp. 9–10.)

These comments apply not only to the memoirs of the High Command, but also to such books as *Company Commander* by Charles D. MacDonald, a former captain of an infantry company of the Second Division. MacDonald's account, like some better novels about World War II, gives a vivid picture of his experiences, but there is no way of knowing to what degree valid generalizations may be formulated from such books. And Marshall's work is only the product of one man's investigation of a vast and complex subject. Useful as many of his observations are for the purposes of this study, his presentation still does not provide data carefully collected under controlled conditions and validated according to standard procedures by teams of analysts operating together in a program based on clearly defined theoretical concepts.

Comparable limitations apply to another illuminating study of military life. It is a monograph by the Finnish social scientist, Knut Pipping, written in Swedish with an English summary which is entitled *The Social Life of a Machine Gun Company*. Pipping served as a noncommissioned officer of a machine-gun company in the Finnish Army during the Russian-Finnish war of 1941–1944.

While this work is much more systematically done and so more useful than are other accounts by participant observers, Pipping points out its shortcomings in these words: "When, in September of 1943, I began to study the social life of my Company, I had no experience in sociological field-work, and partly because of my lack of experience and partly because of fear of our Army Police, I had no occasion to perform sociometric experiments." (Pipping, p. 247.)

True, in the field of psychological tests and measurements for military purposes a considerable amount of literature exists which does report data that have been scientifically reported and validated. But the principles and procedures which have been developed to pick out from a cohort of recruits the men best suited to be, say, air navigators, are not particularly useful for the understanding of the behavior of an air crew as a functioning group.

There are also some studies of the effects of certain social factors on military performance. Thus the relative age, marital condition, and education of the members of a unit have some bearing on the manner in which the group will perform its military tasks. The Research Branch found that favorable responses about willingness for military service were expressed more by younger men, more by unmarried than married men in corresponding age and educational groups, and more by (at least) high-school graduates than by others in each age group by marital condition. (Stouffer, I:124–125.) The inference is that, if these responses can be taken as clues to military performances, a unit composed entirely of younger unmarried men who are high-school graduates will give a better account of itself than a group of older married men who are not high-school graduates. But since the men of one infantry rifle company tend to show about the same distribution of age, marital conditions, and education as the men in another company, these are not significant variables in the analysis of group dynamics.

Similarly, although the methods of classification and training of Army personnel, the degree of physical and psychiatric fitness of the Army population, and the general cultural background of Americans will have an effect on the level of military performance, they can be treated as "given" conditions for our purposes. And the available studies of such factors do not deal with the effect of the primary group on the soldier's life.

RELATION TO FORMAL ORGANIZATION

For all that we shall be emphasizing the importance of primary group behavior in a military unit, we must stress that this behavior takes place in a *military* context. Army social organization and army culture generally impose certain limitations on interpersonal relationships within the primary group.

Not only is an army a large, formal organization which shares many features of other complex bureaucracies in Western culture, but it is designed to operate with force against a severe and resistive external environment. Whether or not any particular set of men in an army ever operates in this manner, their statuses and roles within the organization are mainly formulated to further this purpose.

All this is obvious enough. It means that a group of army clerks who in all probability will never have to meet dire external exigencies other than those, say, which they confront while working at IBM machines in the fastness of the Pentagon, must nevertheless be organized as though their unit might suddenly be called into action in a combat zone. The command structure, within which these clerks function, applies not so much to their immediate tasks as to the general purpose for which the total organization is set up. The relatively rigid social hierarchy and the accompanying patterns which are used to support and reinforce it rise out of the necessity for a firm, reliable, internal organization within any grouping of men who together must meet and together surmount the threats of a dangerous external environment. As George C. Homans has noted, "The more severe a group's external environment, as with ships and armies, the more stable its internal organization tends to be." (Homans, 1950, p. 430.)

The basic purpose of an army thus brings about a particular kind of subculture and organization which governs the informal grouping of the soldier. Hence, a typical primary group—a set of buddies—in an American infantry rifle company will bear certain resemblances to a typical primary group in an American factory or street-corner gang, but it will also be markedly different from either because of the given conditions of Army life.

One of these general conditions is that the specific culture patterns of army life are more compulsive for most men than those which they followed as civilians, and allow for a smaller range of deviation. And army patterns control both the working and the nonworking hours of the soldier. The minutiae of the daily job are prescribed in detailed technical orders, manuals, and directives, which are issued by higher headquarters and reach the individuals in the group through the hierarchical channels of military authority. As one writer in the *American Journal of Sociology* has noted (vol. 51, pp. 365–366), these regulations may cover such subjects as specification for the size of the head of the arrow drawn on a map, hours of work, proper dress for work of various kinds, size of working shifts, nature of supervision, punctuation in work reports, courtesies to be shown to visiting officers, and standards of cleanliness. In the Navy, another sociologist has written, there are officially correct ways of writing letters, greeting fellow personnel, executing air maneuvers, loading weapons, burying the dead, reporting infractions of the rules, fixing the seating for dinners, hailing a ship from a boat, packing one's clothes for travel, *ad infinitum.* (Page, p. 92.) To be sure, there are comparable patterns followed in civilian life, but rarely are the civilian patterns as rigid, compulsive, and comprehensive as are the military.

Perhaps in greatest contrast to normal civilian social controls, the writer on Army life continues, are the regulations governing behavior off-duty. Recruits during World War II soon learned that the Army established formal control over such matters as hours of sleep, hours of eating, the selection of social acquaintances (viz., directives forbidding off-duty social relations between officers and enlisted personnel), hours during which the trains may be used, frequency of shaving, and the selection of seats in Army theaters. In all, the Army way of life was generally felt to be more rigid and constricted than the civilian way of life.

This is not to say that all soldiers always resent the restrictions of army life. To some indeed, its very circumscriptions provide satisfaction and security. But it is to say that the difference in type and range of behavior which an individual experiences when he becomes a soldier makes his primary group, as we shall see later, of special importance to him.

The patterns of army culture are inculcated early in the military career of a soldier and affect his relations with other individuals from the start. No matter how the members of a unit may get themselves organized in addition to the organizational requirements of army regulations, whatever goals and standards they may set for themselves other than the standards and aims of the army command, they still must operate within the hierarchical social structure and the numbered cultural patterns of the army.

Why an army must have hierarchy and numbered pattern in order to fulfill its basic purpose is well brought out in a chapter of *The American Soldier*, written by R. M. Williams, Jr., and M. B. Smith. They note that a company composed entirely of individual replacements, none of whom are acquainted before the day the unit entered combat, could quickly become a fairly effective fighting organization. This would be possible because the cultural framework of action as well as the social organization necessary to bring the patterns into effect was known to the men. On the other hand, say the authors, a group in which the only basis of organization was that of affective ties and common social values among individuals, none of whom were invested with definite formal roles carrying explicit functions, could hardly avoid initial chaos upon meeting the enemy. Eventually, if the group continued to operate as a unit, leaders would arise and a determinate social structure would take form, but this would be a costly procedure.

Thus, Williams and Smith continue, personal motives and relationships are not essential determining factors for group organization in combat. They do not furnish sufficient conditions, and only in a statistical sense are they necessary conditions for organized effectiveness in combat: officers and men must be motivated to engage in combat to make the organization work, but not all of them have to be similarly motivated, nor must they all agree on details of social philosophy or be bound by ties of personal friendship in order for a functioning organization to exist. "To put it another way, the best single predictor of combat behavior is the simple fact of institutionalized role: knowing that a man is a soldier rather than a civilian. The soldier role is a vehicle for getting a man into the position in which he has to fight or take the institutionally sanctioned consequences." (Stouffer, II:101.)

True and important as this is, it is also true and important that the threat of "the consequences" does not always have the same effect on all groups under any conditions, nor does a soldier always fulfill the ideal patterns of his role. If he did, the army unit would operate entirely and inevitably according to the published rules. No human group automatically fulfills all prescribed formal regulations of its culture and there is considerable divergence between the requirements of the orders, manuals, and directives, and the real behavior of any military unit. Indeed, it appears that when a unit is actually engaged in combat, the personal, primary-group relationships among the men are frequently as important for military effectiveness as are the formal norms of army culture. The "institutionalized role" of soldier brings the man into combat; his role as a friend in a primary group may be decisive in determining how effectively he carries out the formal patterns to which he has been trained. C. I. Barnard has described the relationship between formal and informal organizations in general terms: "Informal organizations are found within all formal organizations, the latter being essential to order and consistency, the former to vitality." (Barnard, p. 286.)

Both types of organization contribute to the effectiveness of an army unit, as effectiveness is measured by the army command. The relation of the informal grouping to the efficacy of the formal unit can well be shown when leadership is considered.

RELATION TO LEADERSHIP

The formally designated leader of a unit is not always its real leader—this is as true in the Army as in other social organizations. Real leaders, to use Homans' phrase, are those through whom communications pass and through whom action is secured. (Homans, 1951, p. 431.) They stimulate, guide, and control the coöperative action of the men toward goals sanctioned by the formal organization.

A company officer is always the titular leader of the *unit*—the men assembled for him and partially organized for him by the formal organization. He is not always the real leader, who controls the coöperative functioning of the members of the unit as a *group*. Company officers may be formal figureheads whose directives delimit the activities of the men under their command, but who neither stimulate nor guide nor control the group's own drive toward officially approved goals. Or they may be real leaders who do influence the men. What sparse evidence is available seems to indicate that such real leaders among company officers are generally those who can establish primary-group relations with the men of the unit, so that the men come to believe that the officer's concern for them and importance to them is greater than that which is contractually specified in regulations. Men who share that belief will then become more than a formally established unit; they will become one group or several coöperating groups which strive to accomplish, and usually achieve, the goals set by the officer more effectively than does a unit lacking such groups. Many observers have commented on how important it is for an army unit that its officers be real leaders.

From the empirical evidence collected by the Research Branch it is clear that the officer's personal concern for his men is considered by the men themselves to be important for effective leadership. A typical comment by an enlisted man, a combat veteran, concerning the best behavior for officers was this: "I'd be as close to the men as possible. Let them know that you are there enduring the same thing." (Stouffer, I:385–386.)

If a company officer is to be a real leader, he has a dual role to play. He must be both the agent of the impersonal and coercive organization and the model for willing, spontaneous, imitative behavior. M. B. Smith in *The American Soldier* has put it in this way: The officer may be regarded as a figure of authority by his men, and reacted to in terms of behavior patterns previously built up from their relations with the father and other authoritative persons. In this role, the officer may be a source of guidance and strength. Probably more important, the officer's behavior may be taken as a model by the enlisted men, who identify with him and try to be like him. This identification is most likely to occur when the officer has their respect and admiration.

In any case, when the soldier modeled his behavior on the officer's, the role the officer chose for himself became important for its effect on the enlisted men. If the officer shared the dangers and hardships of the men, they would then be more likely to do their part, whereas the officer who took no personal risks invited similar behavior from his men. Both officers and enlisted men made it explicit that, in combat, effective leadership had to be from in front. (Stouffer, II:123–124.)

Veteran enlisted infantrymen, describing the characteristics of the best officer they had known in combat, mentioned the officer's helpfulness toward his men and his display of personal interest in them and in their problems, more than any other characteristic. Fearlessness and leadership by personal example were mentioned next in order. (Stouffer, II:134.)

An essential element in the qualities noted as being desirable in an officer is identification between the leader and the led. The individual's capacity to identify with other people and to feel loyal to them is one of the decisive factors in good motivation for combat (and good performance in it), according to Grinker and Spiegel. These authors define the process of identification in the following way.

"By identification is meant the feeling of belonging to, being a part of, or being the same as another person or group of people. . . . Two factors of the utmost importance are fused in the process of identification. One is that the person or group with whom the identification takes place is loved or needed to some extent. The other is that this person or group is in a position of authority and in this capacity makes demands upon the individual . . . At times such demands may be resented, but, because of the love and the need to be loved, they are ordinarily accepted by the individual and *included within his personality* as his superego. As he comes to feel himself a part of the group, such demands are later not felt to be external. They do not seem to be foreign to him or hateful—they seem to exist within himself. Thus a feeling of obligation, a social feeling, is born which, if the identification is strong, is powerful and can overrule all of his selfish, personal interests. The pressure to conform to the demands of the group is almost a compulsion, of which is the individual is largely unaware and probably could not explain even to himself." (Grinker and Spiegel, pp. 39–40.)

It should be noted that identification is a two-way affair. If the men of the unit are to identify with the officer, the officer must also identify with the men. He must show that he intends to share their lot—that he is dependent on them in the sense that their welfare concerns him and affects his actions and sentiments.

The importance of identification in the performance of a unit can be put in this way: For good companies, there must be good officers. Good officers are generally those who take the initiative in setting up identification between themselves and the men of the group. The process of identification involves giving the men the belief that the officer shares in their fate and in their hopes, cares for their welfare and is willing to deprive himself in order to do so, is not exempted from the hardships and dangers which they face.

Thus the Research Branch found that among troops who had not yet entered combat, the proportion who said that they would like to serve under a given company commander in combat varied directly with the proportion who thought that he took "a lot of interest in what his men are thinking." Companies with high morale were characterized by far higher frequency of the belief that they had officers who were "interested" in their men, "understood" them, were "helpful," would "back them up"—in other words officers who induced identification and had other qualities of primary-group leaders. (Stouffer, I:387.)

The ways in which an officer can set up identification may be illustrated by two examples from, as it happens, the Navy. One is described by a sociologist who was himself the commander of a small warship. He writes: "A commanding officer had to do everything possible to see that the men were getting what they rated, and, what is much more important, show that he was doing it, even if it meant carrying on guerrilla warfare with the rest of the Navy. It was unfortunate that sometimes a sharp remark from his own superior officer helped the skipper prove to his men that he was fighting for them." (Homans, 1946, p. 297.) Similarly a medical officer who had served on a destroyer where the morale of the men was particularly high notes: "On very special occasions a can of cold beer was issued to all hands at one meal during the day. The can of beer, though it hit the spot, in itself did not amount to much, but the realization that the Skipper was 'putting his neck out' very far to give his men a little extra pleasure did mean a great deal to them." (Bassan, p. 40.)

The capacities which enable an officer to establish a bond of identification between himself and his men are not necessarily those which can be spotted by one of the usual aptitude tests. This is illustrated by a series of tests developed at the Marine Corps pre-officer candidate school at Camp LeJeune in which the men of a platoon rated each other on various qualities. The research workers found that, of all the various means of predicting successful leadership which were tested, the group opinion of a man as a potential officer yielded about the best single estimate of a candidate's potentialities. The authors note that "an interesting point in these 'buddy ratings' is the fact that they are not related to intelligence as measured by the GCT [General Classification Test] (Army) or to mechanical aptitude as measured by the MAT [Mechanical Aptitude Test] (Army)." (Williams and Leavitt, p. 97.)

This is not to say that mechanical and intellectual aptitudes have no relation to the effectiveness of the officer; all observers agree that an efficient officer must be able to perform the technical aspects of his job well. But it is to say that among a number of men who do have the necessary technical aptitudes, those who will make the more effective leaders cannot be detected by the GCT or MAT tests.

The qualities of behavior which do make for effective leadership are described in generally similar terms by various observers who have been able to study good leaders and bad officers in the real context of military action. The following examples of such formulations, by psychiatrists who studied leadership at first hand, are representative. Although these examples refer to leadership among flying personnel, similar remarks are generally made concerning ground troops.

The leader must be not only technically sound, write Grinker and Spiegel, but strong in character and decisive. There must be no question of his courage, so that the men may become strongly identified with him and from this identification absorb strength. The identification makes all his personal attributes infectious. His ability to make the men surpass themselves, to stimulate them to rise above their usual level of efficiency and courage, must be wisely used. The good leader is demanding of his men and gets more out of them not only because he communicates his own strength, but because he asks for and insists upon superior performance. Naturally, he is more likely to get such a performance in combat if he makes the same demands on himself, thus perpetuating the identification. The leader who demands a sacrifice from his men which he is not willing to make for himself is not likely to get a good result. Nothing is worse for morale, these observers testify, than a leader who leads from the safe rear. This completely destroys the personal basis upon which the motivation of American soldiers rests, and stimulates a resentment which is likely to color the whole future military career of the man and his unit.

At the same time, Grinker and Spiegel continue, the leader must have good judgment concerning the limit of tolerance the men have for combat conditions. He must demand results in order to get them, but, if he demands too much and drives the men past their tolerance, their spirit may break. He must also avoid the opposite fault of not demanding enough. A leader may become too strongly identified with his men, be incessantly worried about them and hesitate to ask them to go through repeated hardships and sacrifices. The seasoned leader knows how to avoid the twin evils of too much and too little consideration. This judgment entails maintaining a delicate balance, especially if reverses are met with. Yet it has again and again been demonstrated to what incredible length of sacrifice and effort the men willingly go for a leader who has their confidence and affection. (Grinker and Spiegel, 46–47.)

In summarizing the qualities desirable for a squadron leader in the Royal Air Force, Air Vice-Marshall Sir Charles P. Symonds and Wing Commander D. J. Williams, both medical officers of great experience, present much the same picture. The efficient squadron leader, they note, must have had operational experience and should quickly show himself to be an efficient operational pilot. He ought occasionally to go on difficult raids, and should also go out when losses are heavy or morale low. In operations he should always set an example: "He should fly just enough to be one of the lads and to share their hazards." His interests must be centered on his squadron, he must have plenty of initiative and drive. He is expected to have a personal knowledge of all crews, and to mix freely and be friendly with them. These authors note that the leader should be accessible to the crews and listen to them when required to do so. But he must not appear too sympathetic and kind and in all matters connected with flying must be fair and exert discipline, not giving an inch where duty is concerned. (Air Ministry, p. 53.)

What these sketches of the "real leader" come to is that he must be technically competent, must identify with his men but not overidentify, and in general must conform closely to the ideal patterns recognized by the men. The latter qualification is the same as that which Homans italicizes as a fundamental hypothesis (using the term "norm" as we use "ideal pattern") : *The higher the rank of a person within the group, the more nearly his activities conform to the norms of the group.*" (Homans, 1950, p. 141.)

Gap between leadership ideal and reality.—Now it will be noted that these empirically derived formulations for effective leadership are not really different from the patterns for officer behavior as they are formally prescribed in various manuals and guides for officers. But there is a considerable difference between the actual behavior of officers and the ideal patterns of either the manuals or the empirical observers.

This fact is thus stated by the analysts of the Research Branch: "While it can be argued with some justice that army doctrine and especially army tradition and practice are ambivalent and at points self-contradictory on the matter of officer–enlisted man relations and leadership practices, it seems clear that pictures of the ideal officer which can be constructed on the one hand from enlisted men's comments and on the other from official army publications are closely similar. Yet the volume and persistency of volunteered complaints on this subject provide impressive evidence of the wide gap between the ideal and the performance." (Stouffer, I:388.)

Enlisted men frequently react as did the soldier in the Persian Gulf Command who wrote on a questionnaire: "Officers have not the training to handle men in the correct way. Here is what they should remember: Men are human beings and not beasts and I expect to be treated like a man." And some observers agree with the sociologist who wrote: "In sum, officer–enlisted man relations must be counted as a negative element in the balance sheet of morale in the American Army. American soldiers feel that they are trying to do their job in spite of their officers." (Stouffer, I:388; Rose, 1945, 416.)

During World War II these relations were particularly bad in relatively inactive overseas theaters, such as the Persian Gulf Command. Identification between officers and men was at a minimum in these theaters and surveys revealed a smaller proportion of favorable attitudes toward officers in them than in any other areas studied. And the general expression of unfavorable attitudes toward officers, as we shall note again later in this section, meant more than just the traditional griping by soldiers. It was an index of those units which were relatively inefficient in the performance of their military tasks.

In these zones there was a great gap between officers

and men in opportunities for the enjoyment of scarce privileges; the greater this differential grew the more critical were the enlisted men of the officers. Conversely, where the circumstances of the situation made for more equal access of privileges, generally because all were equally deprived of them, there the attitude of enlisted men toward their officers was more favorable.

This may be the reason for the unexpected results of a study of four Army posts in the United States. Two of the worst and two of the best posts from the standpoint of general living conditions were selected by the Research Branch for study. It was found that there was remarkably little difference among the four in the morale of the men, in attitudes toward their jobs and toward their officers. The director of this study wrote: "All in all, I would say that the men at Camp D (one of the two worst posts) had better morale than they had any reason to have, purely because of excellent leadership." It may be that the excellent leadership at Camp D was a good result of the bad living conditions, which were bad both for officers and men and so were conducive to equality of deprivation and mutual identification between the two groups. (Stouffer, I:364, 181, 354–355.)

The identification between the group and its formal leader, so necessary for effective unit performance, was most readily and frequently established under conditions of combat. There the situation itself enforced the kind of equality which encourages the establishment of patterns of identification among soldiers. We shall examine this process more closely in a later section of this survey, but it is pertinent to cite here some comments of the Research Branch analysts. "The fact that combat soldiers had more favorable attitudes than others toward their officers could be attributed in part to the opportunity to discharge their aggression directly against the enemy. But this would be much too simple a view of the matter. Among combat troops, whether air or ground, officers and enlisted men shared the common experiences of deprivation, danger, and death. Social differentiations and special privileges were at a minimum." Similar observations are made in another section of the Research Branch report. The analysts note that the combat situation itself fostered a closer solidarity between officers and enlisted men than was usual in the rest of the Army. The makeshift character of front-line living arrangements meant that the contrast between provisions for officers and enlisted men was at a minimum; formalities were largely abandoned. Also, combat exigencies undoubtedly led a larger proportion of officers to try to exercise leadership rather than mere command, although the latter might do well enough in less critical rear assignments. (Stouffer, I:367–368, II: 119.)

Leadership difficulties of unit officers.—But the leveling of privilege and the sharing of hardships between officers and enlisted men do not automatically transform mere company officers into real leaders. Such leveling does foster the establishment of identification, but does not guarantee that it will come about. And more is involved in effective leadership than good rapport with the men, important though that is. The leader must be motivated to assume the extra responsibilities and special dangers which leadership entails. The rewards of special privilege, extra pay, and pride in official position are the traditional means of enhancing the motivation of men to be leaders. These are undoubtedly necessary in some degree if leaders as well as officers are to be properly trained and motivated. However, the evidence indicates that the training methods used to inculcate a sense of distinction and pride in official position have tended to hamper the effectiveness as leaders of those who became officers.

A useful, though perhaps overdrawn, account of the psychological meaning of officer training is provided by one of the Research Branch analysts who had gone through an officer-candidate school. Although his description may be fully true for only a few of the more sensitive officer candidates, many had something of the same psychological experience. He says that the candidate is subjected to a nearly catastrophic experience, which breaks down to a great degree his previous personality organization. His former values are no longer valid, and in order to find a basis for self-respect he must adopt new standards or escape from the field. Escape is ruled out because of his high motivation to become an officer. "The catastrophic experience provides a kind of purgatory, a definite demarcation from the candidate's enlisted incarnation that puts a barrier between a new officer and his enlisted memories. It has some of the characteristics of a conversion experience, or the ordeal of a medieval knight." (Stouffer, I:389–391.)

According to this account another mechanism used to form the "officer personality" is the passing-on of aggression. In the course of the ordeal which the candidate undergoes he builds up a fund of repressed aggression. By the time he is in the upper class of the officer-candidate school and especially when he has become an officer, he can take advantage of his higher status to express some of this pent-up aggression. To feel himself a man again and to reduce his insecurity, he seeks aggressively to assert his superiority over someone else. Hence he is likely to assume an autocratic role, in accordance with traditional army structure. The new officer, the account says, somewhat insecure and perhaps a little guilty at his favored status, reactively asserts his status, and finds in the officer-candidate school a justification for his new prerogative.

We may note that this experience, whether it is felt as an ordeal or not, with its emphasis on the distinctiveness and desirability of being an officer and with its attendant anxiety, contributes to making it difficult for the officer, when he must be a leader as well as an officer, to put himself in the enlisted men's role in dealing with their problems.

The net effect is that communication between the officers and men of a company is hampered by this aspect of the officers' training. Unit officers in World War II found it difficult to know what their men were thinking, and many, especially in combat, needed to know. Without such knowledge, an officer did not find it easy to get maximum military effectiveness from his unit. The upward channels of communication which are formally established, such as those provided by chaplains and by the Inspector General's Department, did not serve the required purpose.

This difficulty of communication is a problem which pervades all U.S. armed services. It has been well formulated by Homans, who grappled with the situation as the commanding officer of a Navy ship. Homans says that the skipper must take care of the crew in those matters which they consider important and not simply in those which he (or the Navy) considers important. "How can he tell what these matters are? How can he tell what pressures are building up that may threaten the balance of the organization? To put the matter more simply, I think that an honest commanding officer would be devastated by an effort to answer the question: 'What do I know about the crew?' Without the score, he may play well by ear, but he cannot be sure he is doing a good job in building morale." Homans continues that it was generally recognized in the Navy that a man who took his troubles to the chaplain took them, in effect, outside the organization. If a man was irritated by something in his Navy experience, it was a common joke to offer him the chaplain's address.

It is not enough for the captain to announce that his door is always open; the prestige that surrounds him will prevent most sailors from crossing the threshold. "It is essential that at every level of the organization men should be trained to listen with interest and attention, and without interrupting, to everything their subordinates are trying to say, trained also to fit what they hear into some relevant picture which they in turn can communicate. I do not know whether anything of this sort can be built up. I do feel that something of the sort is required if the commanding officer is not simply to play by ear in the matter of morale." (Homans, 1946, pp. 298–299.)

Leadership position of noncommissioned officers.— According to regulation and tradition the senior noncommissioned officers of a unit have access to the ear of the unit commander and serve as his source of information about the men as well as his channel of communication with them.

Noncoms also serve the enlisted men in presenting their point of view to the officers. They exercise a great deal of direct authority, both as agents of the officers and in their own right, and share with their officers a good deal of the responsibility for the success of their unit.

These factors might be expected to give the noncommissioned officer the same attitudes as those of his commissioned officer. "But he was still an enlisted man," the Research Branch analysts point out, "and was subject to most of the inequalities of enlisted status. Moreover he lived and worked among his men and as a member of the enlisted class was subject to all the continuous informal pressures of other enlisted men—pressures which often were directed against the officer class and official army policies." For the most part the noncommissioned officer reacted to these informal pressures and to his continued membership in the enlisted class by adopting enlisted-class attitudes.

This alignment by noncoms is illustrated in a study made by the Research Branch, in which the officers and men of two combat engineer regiments were asked a series of specific questions dealing with the behavior of the non-com on the job. The answers clearly showed that officers, in viewing the noncoms, had a different frame of reference than the privates. The noncoms themselves gave much the same questionnaire answers as the privates. In this study twenty-one patterns of behavior about which there was disagreement between the officers and the privates were formulated. In sixteen of them, the noncoms tended to align themselves with the privates; in five of them with the officers. Thus privates and noncoms were more likely than officers to approve noncom behavior which involved intimate social relations with the men, lenient interpretation of rules, sympathetic indulgent policies in the supervision of their men, and lack of emphasis on formal status differences between themselves and their men.

The noncom is very susceptible, the Research Branch observers note, to informal group pressure, whereas the officer is fairly well removed from social pressure on the part of the enlisted man under him. The noncom finds himself in a situation of conflict involving, on the one hand, official responsibility to his officer and, on the other, unofficial allegiance to the other enlisted men. It is probably easier for the noncom to give way to the internal social pressure of the enlisted group and to avoid conflict with his officers by diplomacy and outward obedience than to accept the official point of view and be in continuous conflict with his social group. Several Research Branch ·studies show that most noncoms did follow the demands of their informal group rather than carry out the official army requirements when there was a conflict between the two. (Stouffer, I:401–410.) This subordination of formal rules to pressures by the primary group is a factor which shall be considered at greater length below.

It should be noted that these observations apply to line noncoms in a functioning unit and not to drill instructors or cadremen in charge of recruits. Concerning the latter, there is little need for identification between the veteran noncoms and the new recruits, nor can the recruits exert pressure on the noncoms readily. The importance of such noncoms is described by one writer out of his own experience. "In the marine corps, during boot camp, the DI (drill instructor) is almost the recruit's sole contact with discipline, toughness, and power." Their stock remarks, such as "I am not telling you to steal, but no marine ever goes without," made by a man who is "the embodiment of the military oligarchy to a recruit startled into terror and devotion, are taken seriously indeed." (White, p. 429.)

But in a regular company, the noncoms occupy no such lofty and unassailable positions, although the top-ranking ones, especially, have considerable power over the other enlisted men. The noncom's role of intermediary between two opposing social groups is frequently not easy. There is a study which offers some evidence of the heavier mental strain born by noncoms. An Army psychiatrist, analyzing a series of mental cases among enlisted men, concludes that in his sample the proportion of service-connected psychiatric disability was greater for sergeants than for other enlisted men. He suggests that situational factors (those connected with being a noncom) rather than historical ones (those concerning the personal background of the patients) were more important causes of psychiatric disability in sergeants than in other enlisted men. (Frank, p. 103.)

Good evidence is lacking which would indicate whether noncoms are more important than officers in bringing about unit effectiveness, or which would indicate under what conditions one set of leaders is of greater importance than the other. But some Research Branch data suggest that in combat the officers are generally more important. E. A. Shils writing in the Merton and Lazarsfeld volume has commented on this tentative suggestion by the Research Branch writers that the soldiers' readiness to fight seems to be more dependent on their confidence in their immediate officers than on their noncommissioned officers. Shils says that if this is so, it would be in accord with a working hypothesis which states that in the personal relations of subordinates with two levels of authority, affection and trust will go to the higher level while the more proximate level, which is the immediate agent of deprivation (emerging from decisions at remote reaches of the organization), will receive "somewhat more negative affect." (Stouffer, II:130; Merton and Lazarsfeld, p. 34.)

It is clear, however, that the attitudes of the men of a unit toward their noncoms are highly correlated with their attitudes toward the company officers. Companies which performed well in and out of combat had more favorable opinions of both their officers and noncoms than did units which performed poorly. Amply demonstrated by the Research Branch analyses is the fact that the enlisted men's attitudes toward their unit leadership tended toward consistency, and that positive attitudes toward noncoms, like positive attitudes toward officers, were part of the empirical picture of good combat motivation. (Stouffer, II: 128–130.)

It must be noted that questionnaire results are not to be naïvely interpreted as being predictive of behavior. Attitudes revealed in a questionnaire may or may not indicate what course of action will be followed in a real, rather than a pencil-and-paper situation. Here, the attitudes toward officers which are reflected in questionnaires do turn out to be predictive of performance. Evidence from other sources, as well as from questionnaires, demonstrates that unfavorable responses of enlisted men toward their officers do foretell inefficient performance in garrison and combat. But in a later example, dealing with attitudes toward Negroes in the Army, we shall see that the questionnaire results, which were unfavorable to mixed Negro–white units, were not predictive of what did actually happen when mixed units were established.

Diagnostic value of attitudes toward officers.—The men's attitudes toward their officers—whatever the cause of the attitudes—is a key diagnostic feature. Good attitudes mean good unit performance; poor attitudes presage poor unit performance. Williams and Smith, in their chapter on combat motivations in *The American Soldier,* point out that these attitudes were undoubtedly shaped by a number of factors in addition to the objective characteristics of the officers themselves. Some of these additional factors were doubtless in turn causally related to the men's willingness for combat. Matters of personality probably entered into the picture. The data merely establish that "good" attitudes toward officers were part of a favorable motivational complex.

And it is likely that the men's attitudes toward their officers had a real importance in determining whether men fought aggressively and stayed in the fight. "When unfavorable attitudes toward the unit officers developed—whether or not the leadership practices of the officers concerned were the main cause of this deterioration—the formal, authoritative system of controls and the pattern of informal sanctions and values rooted in the men's attitudes would no longer merge in the person of the unit commander. One source of the ties of individual to group would be impaired, and the soldier would be less likely to take extra risks or withstand extra stresses for the sake of his admired leader or in response to his support." (Stouffer, II:127–128.)

Just as our discussion of the formal organization of the unit led to a consideration of the informal group, so does the survey of leadership take us back to this nuclear consideration. Because of his powerful institutional role, the officer cannot be ignored in the informal pattern of attitudes which grow up in a unit. These attitudes invariably polarize around him in one way or another. "The officer who commanded the personal respect and loyalty of his men could mobilize the full support of a willing followership; he therefore had at his disposal the resources of both the formal coercive system and the system of informal group controls. If, however, the officer had alienated his men and had to rely primarily on coercion, the informal sanctions of the group might cease to bear primarily on the combat mission." (Stouffer, II:118.) In other words, an officer who is part of and works with the informal grouping of his men can and usually does lead them in effective performance. An officer who does not have the support of the informal group, has to struggle with his own men as well as with the natural and human obstacles in the way of successful completion of the unit objectives.

To conclude this survey of leadership: The importance of good leadership for good unit performance is a matter of general agreement. This agreement by a variety of American commentators, in itself, is not necessarily significant. For American writers, as the Swedish social scientist Gunnar Myrdal has astutely pointed out, frequently overemphasize the importance of leaders and the passivity of the led in various spheres of social action. (Myrdal, pp. 709–712.) This overemphasis, however, has not led to any great surge of research on leadership nor to the amassing of a body of empirical data and validated generalizations concerning leadership. W. O. Jenkins' review of leadership studies, with particular interest in military problems, found few of significance. (Jenkins, pp. 54–79.) Krech and Crutchfield have noted that leadership training, too, has been neglected in American society. The reasons they give for this neglect, the suspicion of leadership and the belief that leaders are born and not made, are not necessarily in contradiction to Myrdal's observation. For there may well be in American culture both an aggrandizement of leadership and a suspicion of it. (Krech and Crutchfield, p. 430.)

The Army shares these traits of the general culture in that good research studies of military leadership at any echelon of command are few, and leadership training, until recently at least, has been conducted according to antiquated precepts. Officer candidates who heard the maxim "noblesse oblige" talked at them many times and in many ways, have been willing enough to consider themselves a species of nobility, but were not very clear concerning the obligations which they must fulfill to become true leaders. (Stouffer, I:390.)

Although leadership is a subject on which there is usually much talk and few data, there is substantial evidence—such as that concerning the diagnostic value of attitudes toward officers—to support the general agreement as to the importance of the caliber of its officers to the performance of an Army company. There is agreement also on the qualities which a good officer-leader should manifest. But there is a considerable difference between ideal patterns for officer behavior and the actual behavior of many officers. This gap between the rules and reality is sometimes the result of a lack of identification between an officer and his men. Some aspects of officer training impede the officer from establishing such identification easily.

It must be stressed that identification is not a universal password to effective leadership. For one thing, a commander's identification with his men may go so far that it becomes an obstacle to efficient military performance. This is graphically depicted by General Bradley in his account of the First Division under Major General Terry Allen in the Tunisian and Normandy campaigns. Bradley writes that among the divisional commanders in Tunisia, none excelled Allen in the leadership of troops. "He had made himself the champion of the 1st Division GIs and they in turn championed him. But in looking out for his own division, Allen tended to belittle the role of others and demand for the Big Red One prerogatives we could not fairly accord to it." And later: "The 1st Division, under Allen, had become too full of self-pity and pride." (Bradley, pp. 100, 151.)

For all that Allen and his deputy, Brigadier General Theodore Roosevelt, Jr., who was similarly identified with the men, had brought the outfit to a high pitch of combat achievement, Bradley had to transfer them to other posts. The results of their identification, so highly successful on the field of battle, threatened to disrupt the effective operation of the larger units of the corps and army. Evidently Bradley did not believe that either general could shift away from the stress on identification with the men of the division when the situation demanded such a change.

This episode gives the clue to a fundamental factor in effective leadership, whether in a divisional commanding general or in a company commander. The real leader must be able to shift gears, so to speak, in his relations with his officers and men. It has been noted above that the company officer plays a dual role. He is the representative of impersonal, coercive authority and yet is also a soldier who can enter into friendly, noncontractual relations of a primary-group character with the enlisted men. And the real leader must be able to switch from an emphasis on one role to an emphasis on the other, as the external environment or the internal state of the unit warrant.

Homans' general discussion of the relations between superior and subordinate within a group stresses the importance of maintaining the formal institutional role. "Familiarity does breed contempt in this sense, and the advice given to military officers that they will impair their authority if they 'go around with' their men is not altogether unwise." But Homans also recognizes the importance of shifting from one role to another. "Few men are flexible enough to work out a two-stage emotional relationship, òne for the times when authority must be exercised and another for everyday relaxed routine. What is appropriate in one set of conditions tends unfortunately to be followed in all, and, in ships and armies especially, the authoritarian relationship is carried over into situations where it is no longer obviously necessary." (Homans, 1950, p. 246.)

When the "authoritarian relationship" is necessary and when it is a hindrance has been intuitively sensed by successful leaders, rather than empirically analyzed. The process of choosing the relationships, however, is amenable to systematic observation. There have been good laboratory studies, pioneered by Kurt Lewin's studies of boys' clubs, which clearly distinguish two differing constellations of leadership behavior patterns, which have been given the unfortunate, because loaded, labels of "authoritarian" and "democratic." (Cf. Krech and Crutchfield, pp. 423–430.) These studies have not clearly brought out that in a functioning group outside the laboratory, sometimes one and sometimes the other type of leadership is more effective in attaining the goals of the group. This is true from whatever point of view such goals are defined.

The goals defined for a unit by the Army command are also best achieved sometimes by the one and sometimes by the other type of leadership relations. Those detailed to train an assemblage of recruits have traditionally stressed the formal, coercive role of officers and noncoms as did the Marine sergeants cited above. This role is probably necessary in order to transform the recruit into a soldier, although it too can be overdone and defeat its purpose.

Once a company is made up of adequately trained soldiers and, especially, is in an environment of danger or emotional stress, then the more effective leadership relation is that of identification between officer and men. In other words, the men must first become a unit—as the term was used at the outset of this section—and this process seems best advanced when the officer stresses his authoritative role. But once the unit has come into being, then the real officer-leader best increases his identificatory role to foster coöperative group behavior.

There is another shift in leadership relations which becomes effective when the unit is actually in combat. Marshall puts it in this way: "All I have said here should make clear that action requires an abrupt change in attitude on the part of the commander. Prior to combat the touchstone of his success is the interior working of the company; it requires the maximum of his attention. He enlarges his ability to command by advancing his knowledge of the character and potential of his men and by encouraging his lieutenants to do likewise. When he fights, he does an about-face." (Marshall, p. 190.) Then he must concentrate on external operations and leave to his lieutenants the internal working of the unit.

Able commanders have long known not only how to make such changes themselves, but also how to utilize the prevailing characteristics of their subordinate commanders to bring about such changes. This may be exemplified again from Bradley's writing. "I had once agreed in Sicily that Ted's [T. R. Roosevelt, Jr.] easy indifference to discipline would probably limit him to a single star. 'The men worship Ted . . . but he's too softhearted to take a division—too much like one of the boys.' But it was not a disciplinarian the 90th needed now. It called for a man . . . who could give it confidence in itself. With a thick-skinned disciplinarian as his second in command, Ted would have the 90th brawling with the Germans in a couple of weeks." (Bradley, p. 333.)

In a company as in a division, there are times and circumstances when a platoon commander is more effective in the role of personal identification than in the role of impersonal authority. This notion is so apparent that there has even been a cycle of movie scenarios which has presented the theme of the beloved officer who is succeeded by a martinet under whom morale disintegrates until, at a critical and final juncture, the cold authoritarian turns out to have a heart of gold rather than of flint after all.

In sum, under many circumstances the company officer cannot readily be an effective leader without establishing the kind of relation with the enlisted men which has been called identification. Without effective officer-leaders a unit does not usually function at its full potential. The authoritarian role has been readily taught to and absorbed by company officers. The identificatory role is given lip service in officer training but is not easily demonstrated nor well absorbed.

Identification between a company officer and the enlisted men enhances the effectiveness of his leadership because it mobilizes the support of the informal organization of the unit toward the accomplishment of goals officially set. Such identification does not mean that the officer becomes just "one of the boys." Even if this were effective on occasion, the formal organization of the Army makes it virtually impossible. A company officer rarely becomes a full-fledged member of a primary group in the unit; he is rarely as subject to its standards and pressures as are the enlisted men. (Officers, indeed, at every level of rank, have their own primary groupings.)

The description given for this relationship between the officer and the enlisted men of a platoon in the Finnish Army holds true very widely. "Though the men knew their Platoon Commander rather well and, after getting acquainted with him, lived with him on almost equal terms, they always treated him as belonging to a different group, or class." (Pipping, p. 255.)

Identification between officer and men means that the men feel the officer shares some of the standards of the informal group, is not completely impervious to its pressure, and is not opposed to its standards or controls. The nature of these standards and controls, and the general importance of the primary group is our next consideration.

IMPORTANCE OF THE PRIMARY GROUP

As has been pointed out, a primary group in an army company is that set of men who are buddies, who interact with each other more frequently than they do with other men, whose coöperation is greater than any which may be required by their military assignments alone.

The distinction between the closely coöperating group of friends and the formal collocation of individuals is a familiar one in social science. This contrast between the group and the unit made previously in this paper, is similar to that made by such sociologists as Tönnies (*Gemeinschaft* and *Gesellschaft*) and Cooley (primary and secondary groups), as well as by Simmel, Weber, and many other sociologists of recent years. It has been discussed by an anthropologist, Carleton Coon (natural and categorical groupings); it has been made by the *gestalt* psychologist Koffka (psychological and sociological group), by a number of social psychologists, including Krech and Crutchfield (psychological group and social organization) and Jennings (psycho-group and socio-group). (Wilson in Gurvitch and Moore, pp. 141–146; Cooley in Wilson and Kolb, pp. 287–289; Coon, pp. 163–168; Deutsch, pp. 149–150; Krech and Crutchfield, pp. 368–370; Jennings in Newcomb and Hartley, p. 407.)

Several primary groups may exist within each platoon of a company; some may include men from different platoons, but the membership of a primary group usually comprises men from the same company. More definite statements concerning the modal size, changes in composition, and techniques of ascertaining the boundaries of primary groups must await publication of better sociometric data than are now available. Although the membership of the group may frequently change, the patterns of intragroup behavior, the internal organization of the primary group, remain fairly constant. The men of every functioning unit not only tend to cluster in primary groups, but they also develop an informal, internal kind of organization of these groups, consisting of certain standards of behavior, ways of accomplishing these standards, and means of enforcing conformity to them. These standards develop out of personal interaction and are in addition to—sometimes a contravention of—those set by the Army command.

The particular behavior patterns of informal organization followed by a primary group may be shared widely throughout a division or even throughout the armed services, but their actual setting and enforcement is done by the men who work together, live together, know each other, and have come to make similar adjustments to the formal requirements of Army life.

An example observed by an unidentified sociologist at an Air Force base and described in the *American Journal of Sociology* will illustrate the operation of internal organization in a situation involving noncom leadership. A staff sergeant had been noncommissioned officer in charge of a technical ground unit (apparently with considerable independent responsibility) and had been the respected leader of the men in the unit for several months. Then a master sergeant was transferred into the unit and replaced the staff sergeant as noncommissioned officer in charge. The master sergeant proceded to exercise his privileges and perform his duties according to the letter of the formal regulations but erred in that he failed to observe the local standards of the group or to consult with the group. The men of the unit rejected him as a leader and continued to look for leadership to the staff sergeant, even on technical problems which were officially within the jurisdiction of the master sergeant. The article points out that a good deal of tension developed between the master sergeant and the men, and the working efficiency of the unit declined markedly.

We may note that this is typical; when the informal group does not accept the formally appointed leader and resents his attempts at leadership, the quality of work performance deteriorates. The conflict in this instance became so acute that the commanding officer had the master sergeant transferred to another base and reinstated the staff sergeant as noncommissioned officer in charge. The commanding officer's procedure indicates that he came to understand the importance for military efficiency of having the official leader accepted by the informal group.

The article goes on to say that when, several months later, another master sergeant was transferred to the unit, the commanding officer permitted the staff sergeant to continue as noncommissioned officer in charge for several weeks while the master sergeant became acquainted with the local situation and a member of the informal group. The subsequent appointment of the master sergeant as noncommissioned officer in charge was accepted by the group.

One of the most highly valued standards of this informal group, the author of this article continues, was the protection and preservation of each man's right to "off-days" away from the technical work of the unit. When a shortage of trained personnel made it necessary to work more hours, a new official work schedule was posted under which the additional work hours were gained by making work days out of customary "off-days." This was in accordance with official policy, and the new schedule was followed for several weeks. Again, there was a noticeable decline in the quality of the work. Then one man drew up a new schedule which retained the customary days off and obtained the needed extra hours of work by assigning each man an occasional double shift as overtime.

At a meeting of the unit called for another purpose, the men complained to the commanding officer that the new schedule was unfair in abolishing customary privileges. One man said that if the men of the group were again given their old privileges, they would see that the work was done. The commanding officer (presumably understanding that the level of work performance would rise if the requests of the informal group were met) accepted the new schedule as a replacement for the official schedule. In a similar case the official schedule actually remained posted for the benefit of visiting inspectors, but the real working schedule was drawn up by the men and was kept available at the barracks in a foot locker. These instances, minor in themselves, exemplify common processes of behavior in military, as well as industrial and other social units. (*American Journal of Sociology*, vol. 51, pp. 367–369.)

The higher echelon of command had attempted to increase output, but the manner of the attempt had tended to defeat its purpose. This is a not uncommon situation in industry and parallels oft-quoted Western Electric examples. In Homans' words: "The management of the Hawthorne Plant tried to set up the work in the Bank Wiring Room in such a way that output would steadily increase. Instead, the very setup of the work tended to put in motion a social development that partly defeated management's plan." (Homans, 1950, p. 434.)

While a set of men must have some experience with each other in order to develop internal organization, no great span of time is necessary for this development. In the example of the Air Force units, the writer noted that vitality of the informal groups was evidenced by the fact that they maintained their continuity despite a rapid turnover in membership. Individual members were transferred in and out of the unit at frequent intervals without breaking the groups or radically changing their customs. In one technical unit, which was observed for two years, almost the whole membership changed about once every three months. Approximately one hundred different individuals belonged to the group at one time or another during the two years, although the maximum size at any one time was twenty. Status relationships and group standards underwent some changes during the two-year period, but there was never a sharp break. Only on the few occasions when large numbers of men were sent out from the unit at one time were there periods of temporary confusion in the social organization, but the relationships were quickly reëstablished.[1] (*American Journal of Sociology*, vol. 51, p. 367.)

Similar observations, on a larger scale, were made by the Research Branch analysts. They noted that informal controls based on close personal ties and identifications developed among infantry troops in spite of frequent turnover in the membership of informal groups because of the replacement system. "That such ties did develop to the extent observed indicates the strong pressure toward their formation; on the other hand, the fact that such a

[1] This observation applies to replacements who become part of a unit, rather than to individuals who may be temporarily attached to a unit. A pertinent comment on such attached officers or enlisted men was made in a personal communication to the author by David R. Brower whose present duties as editor of the University of California Press were preceded by duties as an officer of the Tenth Mountain Division. "I remember all too well the great reluctance upon the part of members of rifle platoons to accept as an added member in their patrols a man—any man—from the batallion intelligence section. They simply didn't know him well enough."

replacement system could work, with whatever defects, indicates the force of purely institutional controls." (Stouffer, II:104.)

In assessing the relative importance of these informal controls as against the institutional controls, we may note here again—as does E. A. Shils in his chapter on the primary group in the American Army—that the goals for the unit's endeavors and the broad patterns of its functioning are set and controlled by the Army as an institution, but the manner in which these patterns are carried out and the success with which the goals are attained hinge in considerable degree on the internal organization of the unit. (Shils in Merton and Lazarfeld, p. 22.)

Evidence of the importance of the primary group.— The great, sometimes crucial, importance of the primary group for military effectiveness may be seen from various points of view. To the psychiatrist, a typical sign of the militarily useless neurotic or psychotic soldier is the fact that he is not part of a primary group. "The one outstanding trait of all patients admitted to the psychiatric ward was their inability to become part of, and find strength in, the group," writes a Navy psychiatrist. And in another paper he says that one of the most important factors in the rehabilitation of the patient suffering from emotional disturbances induced by combat or operational duty is "promotion of his reintegration with the group so that he may regain the important controls over untoward emotional reactions which identification with the group affords." (Cohen, p. 94; Cohen and Delano, p. 296.)

The problem of social isolation is succinctly put by Homans when he notes: "If there is any one truth that modern psychology has established, it is that an *isolated* individual is sick." And writing of his own experiences as commander of a small warship, the same author discusses the importance of the "segments," the primary groups, among the ship's crew. "The skipper could not, even if he wished, break down the segments into which his crew is divided, and their corporate strength, enlisted in the common effort, will serve him well. What he must do is take care that no one segment sets itself apart from the rest and against them." (Homans, 1950, p. 313; 1946, p. 296.)

When the soldier or sailor leaves the service, his experience of comradeship in the primary group is generally remembered as one of the most valued aspects of his military career. "In fact it is the only feature of the military for which Americans seem to have any nostalgia," writes one anthropologist, and another observes that for Germans as well as for Americans this experience is a significant one whose memory is treasured. (Schneider, p. 297; Spindler, p. 85.)

From the point of view of an analyst of infantry tactics, the primary group is a cohesive fighting force and the breaking up of the primary group may mean destruction of military strength. This is clearly shown in Marshall's study of battle stragglers in the Ardennes operation of World War II. He found that individual stragglers had little combat value when put into a strange organization. Most of them were unwilling to join any intact unit which was still facing the enemy. Some, after being given food and a little rest, did go back in the line. But the moment their new unit came under enemy pressure, these individuals quit their ground and ran to the rear, or sought cover somewhere behind the combat line.

Separated from their primary groups, these individuals had no military value or were even impediments to tactical success Marshall says. "On the other hand, that was not true of gun crews, squad groups, or platoons, which had been routed from their original ground and separated from their parent unit, but had managed in some way to hold together during the fall-back. Upon being inducted into a strange company, they tended to fight as vigorously as any element in the command which they had newly joined, and would frequently set an example of initiative and courageous action beyond what had been asked of them." Colonel Marshall goes on to note that the individual straggler was of such little value that it was hardly worth while attempting to get him back into that battle. But three or four men who hailed from the same small unit and knew one another, would stand and fight if welcomed into a new command.

The difference is, Marshall continues, that these men were still fighting alongside old friends, and though they were now joined to a different outfit, they were under the same compulsion to keep face and share in the common defense. But the individual stragglers were "simply responding to the first law of nature which began to apply irresistibly the moment they were separated from the company of men whom they knew and who knew them." (Marshall, pp. 150–152.)

This behavior was even observed in paratroop operations. Since paratroops must always consider the possibility of a bad scramble during the drop, paratroop training seeks to prepare the men for it. And in airborne operations it is more important than in regular infantry operations to have men who can pick up and go ahead confidently in any fellowship. But despite this training and foreknowledge, the battle morale, willingness, and efficiency of paratroops are in the ratio of their knowledge of the men on whom they are depending for close support.

In a study of some seventy tactical episodes of the airborne phase of Operation Neptune (Normandy), Marshall found only a minor fraction in which success had been achieved despite the disruption of primary groups during the drop. If an officer or a noncom collected a group of men he had never seen before and tried to lead them into battle, the results were almost uniformly unsatisfactory. "The men invariably stalled; the fact that they did not know the others present was to them a sufficient excuse why no action should be attempted. . . They would assemble readily enough under a stranger and they would usually march under him, but they would not fight for him. There were very few exceptions to this rule. . . . It derives from the same mental block noted in the stragglers of the Ardennes—the inherent unwillingness of the soldier to risk danger on behalf of men with whom he has no social identity. When a soldier is unknown to the men who are around him he has relatively little reason to fear losing the one thing that he is likely to value more than life—his reputation as a man among other men." (Marshall, pp. 152–153.)

The importance of the primary group is further indicated, and in more general terms, in a chapter of *The American Soldier* written by Suchman, Stouffer, and DeVinney. These writers comment that few social institutions have such an elaborate body of formal rules and regulations to anticipate all the minutiae of life as does the Army, with punishment specified for infraction. Yet these rules and regulations can be ineffective unless there is "the development of a social climate in which one's *fellows* as well as one's *superiors* serve as checks on a tendency to infraction, and, ultimately, the internalization of the controls [is] such that an individual's 'conscience' inhibits infraction even when there is no likelihood of detection by either superiors or fellows." (Stouffer, I: 410–411.)

But more may be involved in the character of primary-group relations than even the important matter of obedience to rules and regulations. The chapter in *The American Soldier* on orientation toward the war concludes that the general picture given of men preoccupied with minimizing their discomforts, acquiring higher rank or pay, securing safe jobs which would offer training useful in civilian life, displaying aggressions against the Army in many different ways, and getting out of the Army as fast as possible does not suggest a particularly inspired work performance in the American Army. "But Americans fought and fought brilliantly and tenaciously when they had to." (Stouffer, I:485.)

The data available to the Research Branch analysts gave no direct answer to the question of why American troops fought as well as they did in spite of their negative attitudes. But some of their studies hint, as do observations by other analysts (as in the quotation from Colonel Marshall cited above and in comments by Hans Speier noted in the later discussion of typical attitudes), that one of the significant factors in motivating the American soldier both before and during combat was his relationship with his fellows in the primary group.

Reasons for the importance of the primary group.—If all this is so, we must then ask why the informal group is so important. What does it do for the soldier and what does it do to him? The main outline of what it does for him is clear even from the impressionistic evidence which is all that is now available. It gives the soldier a group to which he can belong; it is the one group in which he can get a satisfactory sense of belonging. And men have a strong need for that sense of belonging.

They have that need simply because they are trained from infancy to have it. Most individuals grow up as members of a family group, are taught what they may expect from the other members of the group, and even though they may reject their own family in later life, they can never totally reject—nor do they normally want to—the comfort, security, and satisfaction of belonging to a co-operating, face-to-face group of people. Within that group, the individual knows what is generally expected of him and what to expect from the other members; the interpersonal relations are structured, they follow known patterns. And these patterns of relationship are enduring, pervasive, and compulsive. Their enactment is not limited to specific times and places; they pertain to many aspects of the participant's life; and they are followed despite distractions and altered circumstances. In sum, they are "emotional" relationships, as behavior endowed with such rigidity, intensity, and high value to the individual is usually termed. And emotional ties between persons, Homans has properly pointed out, do not exist in a vacuum but are functions of the activities these persons carry on together and of the ways these activities are organized. (Homans, 1950, p. 277.)

The need for belonging means that most individuals, when bereft of these emotionally tinged relationships, strive to reëstablish such relations with some other person or group of persons. Krech and Crutchfield have put it in this way: "The need to belong to some activity or group larger than one's self, to be 'accepted,' to be part of something significant characterizes most people in society." (Krech and Crutchfield, p. 383.) The Army provides the soldier with a ready-made group and with a vast package of structured relations. But the Army provision is both too much and too little for the soldier.

It is too much because Army culture requires the soldier not only to have certain relationships within his own platoon and company, but also to interact with a vast concourse of groupings, reaching from battalion through division to the misty reaches of corps and Army. He must not only salute his own captain but any commissioned officer who appears on his horizon; he is supposed to have pride, not only in his division, but also in the United States Army. In some degree he typically does have some feeling of belonging to such macrocosmic entities, but the meaningful pride and loyalty, those sentiments which significantly affect behavior, cannot usually be distilled beyond the group of men whom he knows personally.

What the Army provides in the way of social relations

is too little because the myriad regulations pertaining to the disassembly of a rifle or to his duties as ammunition carrier still do not provide him with the support he must have if he is to adjust to such quite commonly felt threats as those presented by his own ambivalent sense of masculinity, or by the sheer uncomfortable anonymity of feeling that he is nothing but a serial number to those who control his destiny.

Not only does the soldier have the need, as do all men, to participate in the life of a primary group, but his need for such participation is heightened by the special strain of army life. Active duty, even under garrison conditions and sometimes especially under garrison conditions (as in the Persian Gulf Command), often involves stresses and threats to the individual which are felt to be greater than those commonly met by civilians. To meet, withstand, and overcome such threats a soldier needs a strength that is more than his own, a strength which he can derive from an informal group whose members together face the same stresses and threats.

And the only primary group available to him must be found within his military unit. Because an informal group is the only possible answer to this dominant need, the typical soldier urgently seeks membership in it, quickly makes this social alliance, and staunchly adheres to the patterns of group conduct. The officer also seeks and forms such alliances. His primary group is made up of fellow officers of about the same rank.

The informal group within the military unit is the only one which can fulfill the soldier's need for group participation and identification because of four general conditions of military service.

First, the individual's pre-Army social participation is weakened and his nonmilitary social status is abrogated. What has gone before in the life history of the recruit is minimized; his adjustment to Army society is of maximum importance. Whatever status positions he may have held as a civilian are usually of little use for his role as a soldier. Commenting on this, one study notes: "The essential fact about induction, reception-center, and basic-training experience is the knifing-off of past experience. Nothing in one's past seems relevant unless, possibly, a capacity for adaptation and the ability to assume a new role. . . The complete severance of accustomed social relations finds compensation in part in the acquiring of 'buddies'." (Brotz and Wilson, p. 374) And a sociologist writing of his observations in the Air Force points out: "The adjustment of individuals to the squadron results in a social system in which status, leadership, clique participation, and value system are based upon criteria different from those found in civilian communities. Socio-economic status, commonly a major determinant in the informal organization of civilian communities, has no effect on status within a fighter squadron." (Stone, p. 388.)

To be sure, this "knifing-off" of previous social participation is not felt as drastically by a chief warrant officer handling invoices at an ordinance depot as it is by a recruit in basic training or in boot camp, but a basic condition of all military rank and service is this general minimizing of non-Army participation and achievement. This is so because of the wide scope of military service in the life of the individual, encompassing as it does so many phases and aspects of all his activities. Sometimes primary-group affiliations made outside the Army must be deliberately abrogated by the Command. Thus Bradley tells of a National Guard division he once commanded whose efficiency was lowered because of cliques among the officers. These cliques or primary groups had been formed in civilian life; maintained when the officers were on active duty, their continued existence tended to foster a favoritism and a carry-over of civilian attitudes which was detrimental to military performance. General Bradley broke up these groups by a complete shake-up and shifting about of the division's officers. (Bradley, p. 15.)

The second condition making the primary group the only one available to the soldier is the fact that the men of a unit are isolated from other social groupings. They have no alternative but to make their social alliances within the unit. Not only are their previous social participations of little account, but present possibilities and future prospects for primary-group affiliation are largely restricted to their fellows in the unit. Frequently enough, this isolation is purely geographical. Military installations are usually far enough distant from civilian centers to make impossible interaction of a primary-group kind between soldier and civilian. And within the military installation, the soldier must spend so much of his time in the company area or the sailor in his section of the ship, that again he does not have much opportunity to form and maintain primary-group ties with men outside his unit. This condition is well stated in the analysis of a fighter squadron. "It must be remembered that a squadron represents the total social, economic, political, and educational world for the individual member. Most, if not all, of his time is spent within the physical limits of the squadron 'area'. The squadron status system pervades everything he does, as there is no way to get away from it. All activities are carried on within the limits of one small organization, in contrast to civilian life in which any single individual may belong to many different organizations. Because of this all-enveloping nature of the group, the adjustment of the individual is not a partial one to only one aspect of the day's activities. Rather, adjustment must be made to a 'total social situation'." (Stone, p. 391.)

In Navy units observed by a sociologist who was a Navy officer, increased physical isolation of the unit brought about increased potency of the informal organization.

On one island air base where there was no native population and almost no contact with persons outside the Navy,
the unit's social structure underwent a major change from
what it had been in the United States. "In this case the informal structure had almost lost its private sanctification
and stood, in large measure, as the officially recognized
pattern of this group of temporary island residents." Although one visiting officer described this as a breakdown
of organization, the unit had high morale and effectively
accomplished its mission. (Page, p. 91.)

The isolation is not only one of space and circumstance,
but also of time, especially in combat areas. For many
soldiers only the here and now is important; plans or
preparations for the future are not very significant. One's
present associations are all-important while deferred
satisfactions of future participation in civilian primary
groupings are not enough to stave off the need for present
group identification. One writer has noted that, in the
Army, time has only a present phase. Thus money has
only its immediate goods and services value. It is used
or loaned or gambled away with considerable abandon.
The future can and will take care of itself. (Brotz and
Wilson, p. 375.) Similarly future associates and associations, probable and attractive though they may be, cannot
substitute for present comrades.

The social insulation of the military unit is pointed
up in the description of the Air Force technical unit mentioned above. There, the informal group included almost
every member of the formal unit. "Personal contacts were
so frequent that men learned to know each other as well
in a few days as they might in a few years as civilians.
There were practically no competing or overlapping
groups; all significant social circles were coincident with
the small group." (*American Journal of Sociology*, vol.
51, p. 367.) There are no other groups to distract the
individual's attention from his informal group in the unit

nor to dilute his loyalty to it. This reason why the primary group exerts so powerful an influence on the soldier tallies with Homans' generalization that "the effectiveness of the control a group exercises over its members is influenced by the social and physical opportunities open to the members for escaping from the group." (Homans, 1950, pp. 289–290.)

Third, the soldier's life is so different from that of a civilian that he finds little continuing support and security in civilian primary groups and tends to debar himself from participation in them. This is not to say that the soldier does not identify with his family or is indifferent to rejoining his family. The satisfactions afforded within the family are felt to be incomparably greater than those of the informal group within the unit. But the conditions of military service frequently preclude normal family life, and the primary group of the unit must substitute in part for it. Indeed, it is more than coincidence that several writers refer to the company as the family unit of the army. For the soldier has a good deal of the same identification with the members of his primary group as he has with the members of his family.

The common experiences and the common stresses of military service are so pervasive in the soldier's life and so unique to his life, that he finds little interest in civilian primary groups or little incentive to join them even if he has the opportunity. The very intensity of interpersonal contacts within the unit fosters firm primary-group relations. All members of the primary group live together in the same section of the barracks, eat together, use the same latrine, take physical training and drill together, work together, go to the movies together, and share almost every other aspect of Army life. This closeness may become irksome, and under some conditions may even disrupt the group. But under most military conditions the constancy and intensity of these relations make for group cohesion.

Hartshorne has indicated how the architectural plan of a girls' college dormitory serves to enhance the authority of the group's opinion. In parallel manner the architectural plan of the Army unit's common mess and barracks makes for frequent interaction and heightening group solidarity. (Hartshorne in Wilson and Kolb, p. 292.)

Finally—in this listing of the reasons why the primary group within the unit is so important to the soldier—there is the fact that he is immediately dependent on and responsible for the other men in the unit, and is usually neither directly dependent on nor responsible for anyone outside the unit. Primary groups exist for personal interaction and because of it. Again, the conditions of military life not only limit a man's personal contacts outside the unit, but they also make the relations within the unit of great importance to him. Much of the soldier's work must be done as team work. The success of his own efforts, whether as one of a mortar team or as one of a loading detail, depend in large part on his team mates.

Perhaps even more important than dependence is the responsibility the soldier has for the welfare of his comrades. They are dependent on him, just as he is dependent on them. If he does not deliver the mortar rounds regularly, the whole team may fail; if he misreads the wind velocity, the whole forecast may be wrong. The personal security that comes from this sense of responsibility has never been thoroughly defined, but it is indicated in a sociologists's account of the experiences which await a new naval officer first setting out to sea. "The isolation of a ship at sea and the consequently heightened desire for acceptance by the social group has never been described (to him). A new man has never been awakened to stand a lonely night watch where the lives of 500-odd men may depend on his alertness." (Berkman, p. 384.) To sum up, another reason why the face-to-face group within the unit is the only one available to the soldier is that within it go on the most intensive personal relations which he experiences as a soldier.

While these four conditions of military service make the primary group within the unit a factor of special potency in the life of the soldier, this group shares the principal characteristics and functions of primary groups everywhere. Thus Kingsley Davis states that "physical proximity, small size, and long duration are the conditions most favorable to the development of intimate ties." And these ties within the primary group constitute a relationship between persons which is "noncontractual, noneconomic, nonpolitical, and nonspecialized. Instead it is personal, spontaneous, sentimental, and inclusive." (Davis, p. 294.)

This recounting of what the primary group does *for* the soldier—how it meets certain of his needs—also tells something of what it does *to* him—how it affects his activities as a soldier. It enhances his security, reduces his fear, and also helps motivate him to do his job both in garrison and in combat. The informal grouping within his company can have this effect on the soldier, partly because within it he can have personal identity, he can "enact a personal drama," as a psychiatrist has put it, rather than be manipulated merely as an anonymous serial number and only as the carrier of an MOS (military-occupation specialty) code number. Being known and treated as a person rather than as a number is a comforting thing for most American individuals, who tend to feel thwarted and powerless if most of their social relations are of a contractual, specific kind. Within the primary group the soldier finds over-all emotional support and not merely aid tendered as fulfillment of a formal or reciprocal obligation. (Coleman, p. 223.)

Several of the large-scale studies conducted by the Research Branch attest that participation in a primary group reduces fear—both in training and in combat. This evidence has been appraised by E. A. Shils who writes that "one of the important functions of the primary group, as *The American Soldier* amply testifies, is the reduction of fear. We have already cited the soldier's own conception of the importance of his feeling of responsibility to his comrades in execution of what becomes in a well-led unit, a primary group goal as well as an authoritative command. . . .

"Primary group relations help the individual soldier to bear threatened injuries and even death by increasing his self-esteem and his conception of his own potency." (Shils in Merton and Lazarsfeld, pp. 26–27.)

One Research Branch survey which reflects the importance of the primary group to the soldier was made when the fighting of World War II was over. The troops overseas were at a relatively low point of personal motivation for military tasks and probably operated at a relatively low level of efficiency. This survey made it clear that although many of the usual pressures and motivations of military life had thus lost some of their efficacy among the troops, the potency of the primary group was not impaired. The troops were asked several questions to find out how important the opinion of the others in his outfit is to the soldier. Nine-tenths of the enlisted men agreed that most soldiers care a great deal about what the rest of the men in their outfit think of them. Both officers and enlisted men agreed that the enlisted man is usually more concerned with what other enlisted men think of him than with what his officers think of him. This implies, as the analysts point out and as other kinds of evidence would probably substantiate, that in any conflict between the officers and the primary group, the soldier's inclination is with the group, not with the officers. And it follows that if the others in the group support an order, the soldier will be in an untenable position in not obeying. If the group as a whole does not support an order, he will be in a weak position if he is conspicuous in obedience. (Stouffer, I:418.)

One of the Research Branch analysts, M. B. Smith, has summarized the functions of the informal group for combat motivation; his formulation applies to noncombat situations as well. He writes of the informal group (the italics are his) that "it *set and enforced group standards* of behavior and it *supported and sustained the individual* in stresses he would otherwise not have been able to withstand. These are related functions: the group enforced its standards principally by offering or withholding recognition, respect, and approval, which were among the supports it had to offer, while the subjective reward of following an internalized group code enhanced an individual's resources for dealing with the situation." (Stouffer, II:130–131.)

We have already considered the support given by the primary group. It is well here to take note of the first-mentioned function, that of setting and enforcing group standards. By "group standards" are meant those ideal patterns or norms from which relatively little deviation is permitted by the members of the group. They are the mores—ideal patterns which are usually fulfilled in considerable degree.

As a participant in a primary group, the soldier is more than a passive recipient of personal satisfactions—he also helps meet the social needs of the other participants. He both fulfills the patterns of behavior set by the group and helps maintain compliance to them. Here, then, is another facet of what membership in a primary group does to the soldier: it directs his behavior to certain typical patterns which are not ordained by the military command, and induces him to enforce conformity to these patterns on any of his fellow soldiers who may violate them.

The attitudes and patterns sanctioned by such informal groups have not been systematically described, but the literature affords some notion of their nature. One of these attitudes most general in scope and most pervasively held among troops concerns masculinity. The ideals of manliness involved are those common to American culture, but they acquire special significance under conditions of military service. Be a man! This precept is impressed on the soldier in manifold ways, and most effectively by his fellows of the primary group.

Concepts of masculinity, as M. B. Smith notes in the passage of *The American Soldier* just cited, vary among different American groups, but a core is common to most: courage, endurance, toughness, lack of squeamishness when confronted with shocking or distasteful stimuli, avoidance of display of weakness in general, reticence about emotional or idealistic matters, and sexual competency.

The conditions under which these notions are applied have changed as between World War I and World War II, says Smith. In the later war there was much less community pressure on the young men to get into the Army. The general attitude was that everyone should do what was assigned him as well as he could, but it was *not* considered essential that the individual "stick his neck out." It seems that the test of social manhood began much farther from the actual fighting in World War I than in World War II. In the first war a man was more severely censured for failing to enter the armed services; in the second war the test was more nearly whether he adequately filled his role once placed in the combat situation. Smith goes on to note that the fear of failure in the role of being a soldier could bring not only fear of social censure on this point as such, but also more central and strongly established fears related to sex-typing. If a man failed to measure up as a soldier in courage and endurance he risked the charge of not being a man. And this is a dangerous threat to the contemporary American male personality. The general permissive attitude toward expression of fear mitigated the fear of failure in manliness, but did not at all obviate it. A man could show and admit fear without necessarily being labeled as a "weak sister," but only as long as it was clear that he had done his utmost. (Stouffer, II:131–132.)

The importance of living up to the standards of masculinity is also described in another chapter of the Research Branch writings (by E. A. Suchman, S. A. Stouffer, and L. C. DeVinney) in which the psychological state of the recruit is described. "The individual recruit is powerless. He finds solace in the company of his fellows, who are new and bewildered like himself, but who now, with all escapes blocked by fear of formal punishment, further each other's adjustment to the inevitable by supplying sanctions of their own to those who 'can't take it'. The fear of being thought less than a man by one's buddies can be as powerful a control factor as the fear of the guard house." And when the social controls concerning masculinity reinforce the purposes of the formal organization, "the Army has begun to succeed in building a soldier—a process which continues until as much as possible is internalized and automatized in the form of 'conscience'." (Stouffer, I:412.)

Much of GI culture and particularly GI language had exactly the function of asserting masculinity, E. A. Shils comments, in a social organization which required it and which aroused two deep and independent sources of anxiety, homosexuality and death. The male character of the Army accentuated the young soldier's need to prove his

masculinity. "The formation of primary groups strength-
ened this tendency since each member feared both the
subjective and social consequences of regression to the
menacing period of latency." In this way, Shils concludes,
primary groups in the Army, by placing a high reaction-
formative evaluation on bravery and aggressiveness—the
chief values of masculinity—serve the goals of the organization. (Shils in Merton and Lazarsfeld, p. 36.)

Various attitudes and patterns are involved in the
generic notion of masculinity. Thus there is typically a
strong stigma against those soldiers who seem to accept
authority too readily. One social scientist notes that a
soldier who is not verbally resistive to the demands of
authority is considered disloyal to his friends and is
thought to be sacrificing his individuality and dignity. A
number of well-known derogatory terms, widely used in
the army, are applied to such a person. (Frederick Elkin,
p. 421.)

Related to this notion of being at least verbally resistive
to authority, is "griping," the constant verbal complaints
so commonly heard among soldiers. In the Army (as elsewhere also) griping is not a successful technique for
eliminating the sources of deprivation, writes the psychologist Irving L. Janis; the soldier learns very quickly that,
by and large, there is no real gain to be achieved by it;
moreover, the fact that griping is done playfully rather
than seriously indicates that it is not intended to change
objective conditions.

On the other hand, says this analyst, griping is indulged
in so frequently and so persistently that it seems highly
likely that it affords some psychological satisfaction. It
may be that by griping the man asserts his self-respect by
accepting his present life situation only under protest.
"The illusion that he is doing something about the depri-
vational state of affairs is based on the expectation built
up during many years of his past life that verbal com-

plaints are an effective weapon for improving his situation." (Janis, p. 176.)

The components of the masculinity concept are listed by M. B. Smith in *The American Soldier*. Among them is reticence about emotional or idealistic matters. In practice this meant that any expression of patriotic or self-sacrificing motives by one of the primary group was immediately quashed by the other members. Smith observes that this taboo against any flag-waving talk was one of the strongest parts of the informal-group code. This was universal among American combat troops and widespread throughout the Army in World War II. The soldiers believed that any talk that did not subordinate idealistic values and patriotism to the harsher realities of the combat situation was hypocritical. Although the taboo was strongest against idealistic talk to an outsider, it applied also within the combat group. "One may conjecture that tender-minded expressions of idealism seem incompatible with the role of the proud and tough combat man who drew his pride from what he had been through, and that the latter adjustment was of more crucial importance to most men. . . The nature of the situation as well as the code of masculine toughmindedness may thus have combined to reduce the expressions of idealistic motivation to a minimum." (Stouffer, II:150–151.)

Not only did the notion of masculinity check talk about the general issues relating to the war, but there was actually very little interest in these issues among troops. It has been suggested that this indifference made the soldier's situation with the primary group all the more important to him. In a paper on the sociology of military organization, Hans Speier notes, as mentioned earlier, that the composite picture which may be derived from *The American Soldier* leaves no doubt that the soldier had neither any strong beliefs about national war aims nor a highly developed sense of personal commitment to the war effort. Speier writes: "It is indeed exceedingly difficult to understand, on the basis of the research here reviewed, why the American armed forces fought as well as they did. The answer to this puzzling question is probably only in part supplied by the rich evidence contained in *The American Soldier* pointing to the extraordinary importance of the primary-group relations in sustaining the morale. It would be erroneous, I believe, to treat as separate and independent the factor of generalized convictions and that of primary-group relations in assessing the causes of high morale. . . The reliance on primary groups for security and comfort may also have been subject to a great many variations; for example, the individual may have become more dependent upon identifications with his group members or with group leaders, as broader convictions and beliefs have faded." (Speier in Merton and Lazarsfeld, pp. 116–118.)

Nor were the troops in World War II often concerned about what went on in the larger military world. The higher commanders and their policies were of comparatively little importance to the rifleman, certainly as compared with the influence his immediate leaders had on his behavior. "Unless the larger command was personalized by a highly popular individual commander, on the one hand, or unless things were going very badly, on the other, men did not give much concern to what went on above." (Stouffer, II:145.)

Soldiers did have interest in the goals of military action, especially the tactical goals of divisional action. Commanders who made sure that their men knew as much of the general picture as was possible to give them, generally added to the effectiveness of their command. But the problems and personalities within his unit loomed much more significantly to the rifleman than did the plans of the higher echelons.

All these considerations are made specific and given

local reference within a particular primary group. An example of the attitudes held by an informal group is given in the account of the technical ground unit at the Air Force base which has been referred to previously. (*American Journal of Sociology*, vol. 51, p. 367.) The author lists five such attitudes; to the quotation of each we add a restatement in more general terms.

"1. Any noncommissioned officer who turns an enlisted man in for punishment for any but the gravest offense is an informer and an undesirable member of the group." The primary group must present a united front toward the external world of authority and no action by a member of the primary group which is interpreted as a breach of group solidarity can be tolerated.

"2. A man's pass privileges are sacred. Other enlisted men should do everything possible to protect and increase them." All members of the group must protect and defend the rights of any one member. Pass privileges are highly important because they afford a temporary release from the uncomfortable restraints of garrison life.

"3. Social distinctions between enlisted men by rank are undesirable, and men who claim these distinctions are legitimate targets for abuse." Within the primary group, rank distinctions conferred by external authority are minimized. The enactment of this attitude often entails a personal conflict that is widespread both in the Army and in the whole society. The soldier believes, as does the civilian, that no great distinction in privilege and prerogative should formally be made among his colleagues. At the same time, he typically believes that it is good for him personally to climb the ladder of formal status and so separate himself from his colleagues. This is not an uncommon situation in American society. In discussing similar processes among college students, Hartshorne says, "There is pressure for 'success' but too much success brings with it certain penalties, notably increased social distance between the winner and the losers." (Hartshorne in Wilson and Kolb, p. 293.)

The Research Branch studies reveal the common ambivalence on this score. "Just as there were simultaneous and contrasting strains to criticize the status system in the Army and to rise within it, so also there were contrasting attitudes in the Army toward promotion. On the one hand there was cynicism about promotions as symbolic of real achievement, and on the other hand there was recognition that civilians on the outside—one's family or friends, in particular—might view the situation otherwise." There was strong condemnation by the troops of currying favor and playing politics. And yet these means of obtaining promotions were widely practiced. It may be that the most severe strains on the affectional ties among the men of a primary group came about when some members of the group were suspected by the others of bucking for promotion. (Stouffer, I:230, 264–271.)

Distaste of bucking, comments David R. Brower in a personal communication, was not restricted to enlisted men with respect to their own group. They openly expressed dislike of it when observed in their officers; officer candidates (although their very continuation in school depended in essence on their bucking) strongly disapproved of any overexpression of it; and officers who were openly guilty of it got the usual treatment from their colleagues.

The equality generally enforced by the primary group among its members referred only to formal army rank. It meant that one member of a group should not claim or get higher prerogatives merely because he wore an extra stripe. But the group itself created and acknowledged status differentiation among its members. In describing status positions in a combat fighter squadron, one observer writes that the status system, informally established by primary groups on the ground and in the air, is largely determined by the amount of time which has been spent in the squadron and consequently how much combat flying has been done. And status determines the privileges and favors distributed within the group. The use of jeeps, choice of aircraft, and of going to rest camps were some of the matters regulated by the informal group. "No Army regulations state that flight leaders, element leaders, and wing men shall each obey the man one step above them and command the man one step below. Only the squadron commander has truly formalized authority. Yet the status system functions to maintain control over the members to a high degree." (Stone, pp. 389–390.)

"4. It is not desirable to set too high a standard of work performance (at another time, exactly the opposite attitude was held)." This attitude is discussed in conjunction with the next one.

"5. Men who work together should cooperate in whatever manner necessary to get the job done in the manner easiest for the whole group." Attitudes 4 and 5 are the results of the decisive influence of the primary group on the performance of military tasks. Underlying both is the principle held by the men of the group that they must stand together, achieve together, and together share the same goals. Thus if most of the group disapprove of their military assignments then the whole group will restrict its efforts. And the collusion necessary for such restriction enhances the rewarding feeling of coöperation among the men of the group. As Stouffer and DeVinney write in *The American Soldier,* the practice of "gold bricking" was a form of coöperative action all through the war. It was developed into a fine art by some individuals. Enlisted men often participated in this practice as a group, protecting each other loyally with no little skill and shrewdness. It was a manifestation of high morale from the standpoint of the participants' goals, of low morale from the standpoint of the Army command. (Stouffer, I:84.)

Another passage of *The American Soldier* notes that the recruit had to learn to curb his desire to do a job exceptionally well, lest he incur the disapproval of his fellows. One Research Branch writer observes from his personal experience as a recruit: "Sanctions against ambition or manifestations of superiority come from fellow privates... An esprit de corps develops in the group, directed not so much in favor of group achievement—although there is pride in group achievement which is a hangover from civilian attitudes—but against the common enemy, viz., the noncoms or the officers as the case may be." (Stouffer, I:414.)

But when the men of the primary group accept and approve the assignment given by the Army command, then the quality of the work performance rises to maximum heights. This is exemplified in many situations, among them in the technical unit where the five patterns listed above were observed. During one period of several months the membership was stable and an unusual esprit de corps developed. Under the leadership of the noncommissioned officer in charge, the group took considerable pride in proper performance of duties. Men who showed skill and initiative on the job were then held in esteem by the informal group. Under these conditions the efficiency of the unit was very high.

How the primary group enforces its standards.—The foregoing behavior patterns and attitudes are among those typically held and enforced by the informal group. How are they enforced? The primary group has no formal authority, its coercive powers are nowhere described or prescribed. Nevertheless, its enforcement sanctions are as powerful, sometimes even more so, as those backed by the whole panoply of institutional might. The techniques of enforcement are simple and familiar: verbal taunts, the withholding of privileges, and ostracism. Because of the intimacy and immediacy of the primary group, the first two techniques are generally highly effective; because of the isolation of the group, ostracism is dire punishment since the individual has little or no opportunity to join other groups.

In *The American Soldier* there appear excerpts from the diary of an enlisted man which illustrate the primary-group taboo on overt friendliness with authority. "Yesterday, K went up to Lt. C during class to ask him questions. Everyone chorused and made loud kissing, sucking noises at him as he walked down the aisle, which made Lt. C laugh, but K seemed not to have heard. This making of sucking noises is quite the custom now, and is directed at K and S especially... These two people were disliked, and few were friendly toward them, though they were friendly toward each other. This unfriendliness did not go to extreme ostracism, but occasions arose where people avoided their company." (Stouffer, I:266–267.) Merton cites this example to point out the mechanisms of the in-group operating to curb positive orientation to the official mores. And it demonstrates the process through which this orientation develops among those few who take these mores as their major frame of reference, considering their ties to the in-group (primary group), as of only secondary importance. (Merton and Lazarsfeld, p. 94.) Some individuals tend to reject the attitudes of the informal group, but the number of those who can withstand its pressures is small indeed.

How the informal group enforces its standards was illustrated in the description of the Air Force techincal unit. The author writes in the *American Journal of Sociology* that the informal group had many ways to express and make effective its dissatisfaction with official regulations or arrangements, and the most effective of these was the control by the group of the noncommissioned officer in charge. Since he was one of the informal group, he was subject to all its pressures. If he failed to act in accordance with the interests of the group, he would be subject to the usual name calling: "brownnoser," "eager beaver," "chicken."

In this Air Force unit, the author continues, generally even mild social ostracism would bring an offender in line. This was so because failure to be included in the activities and discussions of the group meant isolation and loneliness. The offender had no other social group to which to turn. The whole basis of his social life and status was in this informal group.

As we have seen, the pressures exerted by the informal group also operate to negate or readjust the rights conferred by formal rank, if the rank does not coincide with the individual's place in the status system set by the group itself. In the cited Air Force unit this discrepancy was exemplified by the lack of real power in the hands of subordinate noncommissioned officers. Officially, each shift of workers in the unit was under the management of a subordinate noncommissioned officer, who was responsible to the noncommissioned officer in charge. Actually, however, these noncoms exercised little authority. They were on terms of closest intimacy with the men on their shifts, and this intimacy usually precluded any real observance of the official relations of superior-inferior. The author notes that leadership on the job was worked out informally and was almost as often in the hands of a dominating private as of a noncommissioned officer. The informal-group pressures which influenced the noncommissioned officer in charge were even more powerful in controlling the subordinate noncoms because even their official work relations were entirely within the informal group.

Finally, this example of the Air Force unit illustrates another technique of enforcement used by the informal group—the withholding from an offending member the means of enjoying certain privileges. "For example,

Charley G.—often took advantage of the privilege of taking an extended pass by exchanging duty shifts with another man." But on several occasions Charley returned late from his pass and thus disrupted the work routines. This forced another man to work for him and shortened the pass of the next man to leave. By common consent this matter was not brought to the attention of the commanding officer. Instead, the members of the group punished Charley by refusing to change shifts with him again. This was considered a severe punishment and just retribution. (*American Journal of Sociology*, vol. 51, p. 369; see also Davis, p. 147.)

These techniques of control—of bringing errant behavior by a member back to the former degree of obedience to group standards—are common in primary groups of every social milieu. And the very routine established by a group becomes a means of social control. Thus a fundamental assumption in Homans' analyses of the human group is that interaction with others is rewarding to a person, and failure to interact (social isolation) is hurtful. Such failure is especially hurtful if you have no other group to which you can turn. "The routine of a group therefore implies a control: once it is established you depart from it at your social peril. Conversely . . . even a hint of peril helps establish the routine. If, fearing the consequences of departure from the group's routine, you act so as to abide by it, you have by that action helped establish the routine. Custom and control grow up together." (Homans, 1950, pp. 177–178.) And in the Army, the customs which develop as a reaction against the formal impersonal routine—such as the GI's language—become in themselves a routine enforced by the informal group.

Assimilation into the primary group.—A typical newcomer into a unit quickly learns about the informal-group standards and their enforcement, soon adjusts to the situation, and readily participates in a primary group. The process of assimilation is generally rapid and smooth because the newcomer is eager to form primary-group alliances and the men of the group are willing to accept him if he conforms to their standards.

The manner in which this process goes on among pilots in a combat fighter squadron has been discussed by Stone. He says the most important social device for teaching the new members the values of the group is the "bull session." In the long and protracted discussions and arguments of the pilots one finds expressed all their prejudices and attitudes. In these sessions the new member must learn the elaborate terminology of flying and combat if he does not have full command of it already. Without this vocabulary the new pilot does not become a bona-fide member of the group. He learns that the values of the group are formed around combat experience and leadership qualities, that all noncombat officers are looked down on, especially ground officers, who are called "paddle-feet" or "ground-hounds." And civilians are, of course, the lowest of the low.

The concept of equality within the group, mentioned above, is well inculcated, says Stone. "As differences between college graduates and men with no more than high school education are unimportant in carrying out the squadron missions and as the whole society is integrated around the squadron function, one would not expect a college education to be important in the scheme of squadron values. The fact is that college men get along better if they do not talk too much about their education. Any attempt by a pilot to show that he is superior to his squadron-mates because of advantages enjoyed in civilian life is strongly resented." (Stone, p. 393.) A new pilot promptly learns that he must exclude from his conversation undue references to his undergraduate days at Princeton and include the proper group terms for ground officers.

The Research Branch made large-scale studies of the assimilation of replacements. These studies have been reviewed and assessed by E. A. Shils, and the following summarizes his findings. (Shils in Merton and Lazarsfeld, pp. 29–31; Stouffer, II:242–282.)

In 1944 the Research Branch conducted extensive surveys to compare the attitudes of combat veterans with those of replacements in veteran divisions, and with those of troops not yet experienced in combat. Questionnaires were filled out by veterans in two infantry divisions, by the replacements which had arrived in those divisions, and by infantrymen in three inexperienced divisions. Clear differences in attitude among these three classifications were revealed by the questionnaires.

Concerning the willingness to enter combat the replacements in the veteran divisions approximated the attitudes of the veterans. The totally inexperienced men were most willing to enter combat, the veterans least willing, and the replacements more than halfway toward the veterans. Concerning self-confidence as combat leaders, replacements had less confidence in their own ability than either the veterans who had most, or the green men who were less self-confident than the veterans. In respect to their attitudes toward their noncommissioned officers, the replacements were most favorable, the veterans second, and the green men least favorable. And the replacements were proudest of their company. They were even prouder of their unit than were the veterans, and both were markedly ahead of the green men.

These findings, Shils comments, indicate that infantry replacements apparently felt inferior to the established primary group into which they had not yet or only recently been accepted and which had considerable prestige for them. Prestige accrued to the men of the established groups because they were combat veterans and because they participated in functioning primary groups and so shared intimacies and knowledge. This feeling of inferiority held by the replacements influenced them to value themselves less than did soldiers in inexperienced divisions and to value their superiors more than these green men did. This high evaluation of the primary group composed of veterans into which the replacements had not yet been fully assimilated, gave them pride in their membership in the company in which the veteran primary group was established. Hence they sought to "prove" themselves by taking over the veteran's attitude in such matters as conviction about the war and willingness for combat. On these two issues their attitudes ranked between the other two groups.

According to Shils, these data also show that the newcomers tended to overestimate the degree of solidarity which prevailed in the established group. In units in which the veterans felt relatively little pride, the newcomers were prouder of their company than were the veterans, presumably because the new men had not yet been allowed to share in the primary-group life and so were not familiar with the attitudes of the veterans. Replacements were not usually resentful of their feeling of inferiority to the veterans; they accepted it and were grateful for the help given them by the veterans.

The replacement was typically eager to enter a primary group, Shils concludes, and willing to follow the patterns and attitudes of the group members. If anything, the replacement tended to overestimate the solidarity of the group. The men of the established group, on the other hand, were not reluctant to take in newcomers, unless possibly when replacements threatened to flood the established unit.

Shils offers "a very tentative hypothesis" that the larger the proportion of newcomers, the greater the resistance of the established primary group to their assimilation. In units with larger proportions of replacements, both veterans and newcomers were apt to say that teamwork in their units was poorer than it was reported to be by both newcomers and veterans in units in which the proportion of replacements was smaller. Once taken into the group, the newcomer was as thoroughly loyal and devoted to it as were those who had participated in it for longer periods.

Relation of primary group to formal groupings.—This loyalty toward the primary group is usually extended beyond the company and includes the battalion or regiment and the division within which the primary group exists. This is so partly because the actual primary group has no label and usually no clear-cut boundaries. For example, a soldier may have the closest relations with four of his fellows in the platoon, quite close ties with all but two of the other members of his platoon, and friendly but not frequent interaction with most of his company. At any given moment his primary-group interaction may include more or fewer men. The shifting membership and changing degree of close interaction does not impair the operation of the group or its importance for the individual, but it does make it difficult for the individual to make clear reference to the object of his loyalty.

The formal entity, whether regiment or division, is an enduring and clearly defined body. Hence the solidarity with the informal group is most frequently expressed as the loyalty to the formal entity, and such expression is part of the informal group code. M. B. Smith, writing in *The American Soldier,* puts it in this way: "Loyalty to one's buddies and more generally to one's outfit was another stringent group code. It is allied to the code of masculinity, but independent in the sense that someone who let his buddies down through irresponsibility, not through cowardice, might not have his social manhood called into question. Loyalty to one's buddies was founded on the fact of vital mutual dependence and supported by a cluster of sentiments grouped under the term 'pride in outfit'. . . While the men's closest personal ties were within their companies, major tactical goals were the achievement of larger units, and the companies in a regiment or division on the whole shared the same experiences." (Stouffer, II:135–136, 138–139.)

The expression of primary-group solidarity as loyalty to outfit and pride in it is further encouraged by specific educational devices in training. These devices stress the difference between the social affiliation of the soldier and other sectors of his own society (hardly ever with another society or with enemy groups). The soldier is constantly reminded that he is not a civilian and should not act like one. The infantryman in training is told, "You're an infantryman; act like one. Don't be sloppy like them Air Corps guys." The Marine in boot camp hears, "You're not in the Army, you're in the Marine Corps" expressed constantly in a hundred different ways. One participant observer has said that rivalry between units is the keynote of Army indoctrination. The Navy is the first target for the spirit of rivalry which then continues, in the Army, down to other companies, platoons, and squads. (*American Journal of Sociology*, vol. 51, p. 377; White, p. 429; Berger, p. 85.)

The effect of reiterating the difference between the individual's branch of service or his division and other branches or divisions enhances internal cohesion and so encourages military efficiency, but there are disadvantages to this practice also. Antagonism thus fostered can lead to limitation of usefulness. In any event, such negative devices are probably not effective unless there are also positive satisfactions, which the men derive from their experience within the primary group.

These positive satisfactions which build and maintain loyalty to outfit are especially derived from the joint achievement of difficult goals by the outfit. This occurs and can be brought about under garrison conditions but it is most commonly and poignantly experienced in combat. Indeed all the relations within the primary group and the effects of participation in it are intensified under stress conditions.

RESPONSE TO STRESS SITUATIONS

When a group of men experience a stress situation together, whether a drought, or a drastic drop in sales, or a common enemy, they often tend to consolidate their efforts and coöperate more intensively than they did before the common danger appeared. Thus Homans has noted that the warmth of feeling between companions may be vastly heightened by their joint and successful operation in a dangerous environment; this tends to make their "interaction especially frequent and sentiment especially intense." (Homans, 1950, p. 117.) It may also favor a starker form of leadership than might otherwise prevail.

This process is well known, but the concept remains an impressionistic even though valid one which must be further refined and checked if it is to have scientific utility. As E. A. Shils says: "It is of course ancient wisdom that groups are integrated more closely when they are faced with an external threat. The data and interpretation in *The American Soldier* have given rise to no fundamentally new hypothesis on this problem and they do not easily help us to refine and make more rigorous the old. But they do bring out certain nuances and point the way toward new research." (Merton and Lazarsfeld, p. 37.) These nuances and research leads which are offered in the Research Branch data and in other sources frame the problem and tell us something of the content within the frame.

Group rewards and punishments.—Thus there is an illuminating discussion of group rewards and punishments in *The American Soldier* which demonstrates that the procedure of punishing an entire unit for the offense of one member frequently does not have the effect desired by the military command and, perhaps more often than not, has the opposite effect. These findings are pertinent to our analysis because they indicate that a stress situation experienced together by a group does not necessarily make for better formal discipline or greater military efficiency.

When 2,881 officers were asked in a Research Branch questionnaire whether group punishment was a good idea, 58 per cent replied that it was never a good idea. While group punishment is explicitly intended to utilize the informal controls of the group to enforce some formal ordinance, it actually has that effect only in certain situations. It was found that group punishment tended to fail in its purpose when it was meted out to a unit because of an individual who went AWOL, or for a barracks theft, or for the failure of one subunit to pass inspection. More effective was the punishment, not of a whole detachment, but of one small group of men because quarters or equipment for which they were jointly responsible failed to pass inspection. If this latter practice was a regular thing it tended to induce the men to react indignantly toward those individuals who failed to do their share in a group task. Group rewards tended to be more effective than group punishments, but were used much less often.

The Research Branch analysts noted that group punishment was most likely to be effective under such principal conditions as these: that the punishment was regular, that the men were able to distinguish clearly between acts which were and were not likely to elicit the punishment, that the men knew that the punishment would affect the entire group, and that the men were able to identify potential offenders in a group and thus be in a position to apply group pressure. (Stouffer, I:423–429.)

And these conditions are eminently met in combat. There the group punishment comes at the hands of the enemy. The men realize that punishment for a violation of effective procedure results in regular and probable punishment, they know that the entire group rather than just the offenders will suffer, and they are able to identify potential offenders and apply group pressure on them. However, in the actual stress of battle, positive motivations are at least as important as the fear of primary-group pressures. To understand what happens here we must consider the nature of combat stress.

The primary group under combat conditions.—For the soldier in combat, stress is a normal situation. In other human circumstances, every effort is made to avoid stress or to minimize it. In battle, the stress is continuous and not easily controlled. "Rather, the intent is to increase the stress continually in the furious pursuit of victory. It is man made, it is intended that way, and therefore it cannot be escaped, avoided or controlled, but only endured." The psychiatrist authors of this comment go on to say that the various factors involved in the physical stress of combat cannot be regarded as independent entities since they mutually reinforce each other. Writing of combat air crews particularly, they say that long flights would not be so wearying had there been adequate sleep the night before. Tolerance for monotonous food would not be so low if the men were not so fatigued. On the other hand, sleep would be less elusive after a full and satisfying meal. The effects of physical stress are cumulative and gather a momentum that can only be interrupted by removal from combat activity. But the most serious reinforcement of the effects of physical stress is the emotional stress of combat. This emotional stress is a complex network of unusual strains inherent in the combat situation. The stress is derived from different sources, which again mutually reinforce each other. (Grinker and Spiegel, pp. 28, 32–35.)

While membership in a primary group is not a sovereign remedy for battle stress, a soldier who fights beside primary-group comrades is more capable of withstanding the stress of battle than is one who does not have such relationships. Under conditions of combat, moreover, when it is crucial that the members of the unit perform effectively as a group, many of the usual techniques of control (such as individual or group rewards and punishments) are not as effective as they can be in noncombat situations. In these conditions of extreme stress, the internal organization and the informal standards of the group assume even greater importance.[1]

They are more important because the factors which make the primary group important in general are intensified in combat. More than ever, it is the only available group for the individual; in greater degree the soldier needs a group; the social isolation, the cutting-off of the past, the interdependence and interresponsibility—all are heightened in battle. Colonel Marshall expresses this succinctly when he writes: "In battle, you may draw a small circle around a soldier, including within it only those persons and objects which he sees or which he believes will influence his immediate fortunes. These primarily will determine whether he rallies or fails, advances or falls back." (Marshall, p. 154.)

Again we must note, as do the Research Branch analysts, that it is important to avoid any one-sided interpretation of the social forces that keep men in combat. The

[1] In the Finnish Army units observed by Pipping, the standards of the primary group were applied to officers in certain instances. "Officers were, of course, expected to show as much courage as the men. An officer who did not follow his platoon in the fire, or who only occasionally visited the line, ran the risk of being shot by his own soldiers during combat, as examples from the First Battalion tell us." And the reason given by the men for enforcing the standards of the informal group in this way was that the formal organization would not enforce them. "The men said that a cowardly officer who drove his men into fire without following them, would always be white-washed in a courtmartial; and therefore they must protect themselves by such drastic means." (Pipping, p. 258.)

various factors in the situation interact. Thus exposure to external threat becomes a unifying force only when escape from the situation is ruled out as it is by formal Army rules and sanctions and by informal codes enforced by the group. "Affective ties binding the group together were important in keeping men in combat because, among other reasons, the group through its formal organization was inextricably committed to the fight: anything that tied the individual to the group therefore kept him in combat... In considering any single aspect of the social situation of combat separately, the fact that it has been abstracted from a most complicated context must be remembered." (Stouffer, II:100.)

Gradient of combat efficiency.—One of the variables in this complicated context is the duration of exposure to combat. The ability of the individual separately and of the primary group collectively to maintain military effectiveness varies according to the length of combat experience. This gradient of efficiency is especially recognizable in air fighting. Grinker and Spiegel note that when flying personnel join their unit in the combat theater, their eagerness for battle rapidly becomes tempered after a few combat missions. "At that point a great strain is placed on their individual motivation. As they begin to realize what they have let themselves in for, it is only natural that they should search their souls as to why they ever allowed it to happen to them. . . . If the weakening of personal motivation were not counterbalanced by some other force, the desire to fight would rapidly diminish. The additional force necessary to keep the men's determination to continue in combat at a high level stems from the effects of the combat group, and is recognized as group morale. It is therefore more than the simple sum of the individual motivations found in the men before they came into combat. It is the result of the interpersonal relationships described in the previous chapter, and, specifically,

of the intense loyalties stipulated by the close identification with the group. The men are now fighting for each
other and develop guilty feelings if they let each other
down." (Grinker and Spiegel, pp. 44–45.) Identification
with and loyalty to the primary group carry the airman
through the first phases of his combat experience, but the
greatest strain on this identification and loyalty comes in
the later phases of his tour of combat duty.

This has been well described in a study of combat crews
in the Royal Air Force. The author of this study writes
that immediately after the beginning of a tour of duty
there is a perceptible rise in morale. This is due to the
feeling of accomplishment, now that the long months of
training are left behind, and to the novelty, excitement,
and interest of this final stage of experience and adven-
ture. But by about the fifth sortie this surge in morale
begins to give place to the recognition of the formidable
reality of the tour. This tends to continue, in some cases
almost subconsciously, until by the twelfth or fifteenth
sortie the man has reached the stage in which the full realization of the danger and unpleasantness of the job have
been forced upon him. Yet there stretches in front of him
an ominously large succession of sorties before he can
achieve the honorable completion of his tour. Indeed,
while seeming more desirable than ever before, this completion now appears so remote as to be an unprofitable
and almost impractical goal on which to pin his hopes.
At this point, when his chances of survival are bound to
occupy his mind to greater or less extent, the airman is
passing through the critical phase of his operational tour.
It is at this point that he needs all possible emotional support from every available source if he is to be able to
carry through to the end of his operational tour of flying
combat duty. (Stafford-Clark, pp. 19–20.)

A similar curve of efficiency has been postulated for
infantrymen. From the evidence of questionnaires in

which veterans rated the effectiveness of their fellows in combat, the Research Branch analysts found a definite peak in combat efficiency. The proportion of best riflemen reaches its peak among men who have been in combat four to five months, after which it begins to drop. The proportion of best noncoms reaches its highest point somewhat later, after six or eight months of combat, after which it falls off. In both groups, men who have had more than eight months of combat time are apparently less likely to be rated as the best men in their outfits. "The main conclusion warranted by the data is simply that combat efficiency appears to reach a peak after prolonged combat experience, after which it falls off." (Stouffer, II:284–289.) This evidence is no more than indicative, but it does indicate that there are stages in the individual's combat experience when he has special need of the support of the primary group—as the RAF airman did between the middle period and the completion of his operational tour. Also there may be stages when the soldier has most to contribute to the effectiveness of the group, as the noncom rifleman in his sixth to eighth month of combat.

There is, of course, great variation in the intensity of the combat situation. The "combat" noted above is of a high order of intensity. Contrast, however, the experience of the Finnish company of which Pipping was a member. It was in the trenches for 16 months without rest in the rear during 1941–1942, and till 1944 was usually three to five months in the line and two to three months out. The average strength of the company was about 150 men. In its four years of combat it sustained a total of 503 casualties (66 killed, 241 wounded, 174 sick, 22 missing). Of the sick and wounded, 290 men returned to the company. This still means a total of 213 casualties over four years. The company experienced intense combat in 1941 and again in 1944, but was apparently still an able fighting unit when it was disbanded in 1944. (Pipping, pp. 253, 259.)

Sustaining and impelling forces.—Some forces which sustain the soldier through all his combat experience, as well as in those phases of his tour of duty when he is psychologically most vulnerable, have already been considered. Not to be neglected among these is the basic institutional authority. Its clear and definite structure prescribes a course of action which can be followed when alternative courses are closed or seem undesirable. Although its coercive powers are not a primary consideration among the men in combat, yet the personal and social consequences of undergoing punishment (in the sense of bringing shame upon one's family) are of considerable importance. The drill and training which the group has undergone is essential to effective performance.

Another sustaining force is the use of prayer. This was especially important to those who had experienced greater stress or who felt greater stress. Those who feared more, prayed more. Other patterns which were adopted by troops in combat as aids in carrying them through the stress periods were various magical practices, attitudes of fatalism and hedonism, and an apathy which the Research Branch analysts call "the strategic abandonment of hope." (Stouffer, II:172, 188–191.)

One of the most fundamental of these sustaining forces, as we have noted repeatedly, is the power and security which the individual gets from his primary group. This he derives in several ways. On a very practical level, the Research Branch analysts write, the soldier can count on being looked out for by his buddies if he is in a tough situation. If he is wounded, he can count on both his buddies and the medics to take care of him. "And at the level of the soldier's immediate combat unit, he was bound to his company for reasons of self-interest in addition to loyalty and pride. The men in his unit were his buddies, whom he had fought beside and learned to trust and depend on, so he felt safer with them." (Stouffer, II:142–143.)

This primary-group affiliation was not only a sustaining force, but was a most important impelling force. It not only helped keep the men in combat but also enabled them to press the attack and so expose themselves to further dangers. This is dramatically reflected in the statements of many combat crew members in the U. S. Air Force that they suffer more when they are on the ground and their crew is flying without them on a combat mission than they do when they are flying. (Grinker and Spiegel, p. 36.) A medical officer of the Royal Air Force writes in a similar vein: "Everyone looked forward to the completion of his tour, but so strong was the crew spirit in bomber command that it was not an uncommon occurrence for a man to volunteer to do as many as ten extra trips so that he and his crew could finish together, if for any reason he had joined them with more to his credit than they had done." (Stafford-Clark, p. 15.)

Such feelings and behavior are a highly specific reaction to leaving one's immediate social group, rather than an expression of a sense of not having done one's share. A pilot who had completed his tour of combat missions, had done his share both according to official standards and according to the informal code. Furthermore, combat troops are often glad enough to permit some other unit the privilege of attacking. "The morality lying behind the guilt reactions of men who were removed from combat was much more concretely tied to the closely knit group in which the soldier fought. The formulation tended to be: 'I'm letting my buddies down—some of them are dead, and the others are still in there taking it, while I'm safe. True, I've done my part, but I have no right to be out of it so long as they are still involved.' " (Stouffer, II:137.)

Many other motivating factors may come into play in any specific combat situation. For example, in a winter campaign men sometimes are moved to attack for the simple purpose of taking a town which promises shelter and warmth. A passage in *The American Soldier* points out that it was no small matter to win a height which deprived the enemy of an artillery observation post, or permitted observation of enemy movements. Indeed anything which gave even temporary and relative safety or comfort, could become a major motivating condition. Tactical victories, those which got something for the unit, rather than the achievement of major strategic objectives, are important impelling forces. (Stouffer, II:171.)

None of these possible motivating forces is indefinitely good in combat. Prolonged exposure to combat inevitably makes for the attrition of combat motivations, even those which develop out of primary-group allegiance. If any one component of primary-group allegiance was stronger and longer lasting under stress than others, it was the factor of responsibility for the safety and lives of others. In the passage of *The American Soldier* just cited, we find this statement: "To the incentives of securing temporary relative safety or comfort, of shortening the war, and of securing material gain must be added, in some situations, certain more exclusively social factors. A good case in point is the situation of attacking to relieve a unit which had been cut off by enemy forces or attacking to recover wounded men. The relief of the garrison at Bastogne during the Battle of the Bulge in December 1944 is an example from the European war. Uncounted smaller actions of the same pattern took place during World War II, and the historical record of past wars is studded with examples. The special motivational feature of such situations for the relieving force is the reinforcement which was thereby provided to the individual's sense of obligation to, and social solidarity with, his comrades." (Stouffer, II:171–172.)

The feeling of responsibility for one's fellows, especially those of the primary group, is evidently a powerful motivating force under certain combat conditions. This is further evidenced by the extraordinary bravery manifested by medical-aid men both in World War II and in the Korean campaign. Although the medics are generally underprivileged in such matters as formal rank, manner of selection for the task of medic, and thoroughness of training, they typically display degrees of fearlessness and initiative under fire not surpassed by combat personnel who are more advantaged in these matters.

The reason for this seems to lie in the special attraction which responsibility for others seems to have for the American soldier, and the favorable challenge which it presents. This is exemplified by Marshall's observation that riflemen who fail in combat may often be transformed into efficient combat soldiers simply by giving them more responsibility. Marshall notes that it sounds like a paradox to expect greater response to come from increased responsibility. "But it works. I have seen many cases where men who have funked it badly with a rifle respond heroically when given a flame-thrower or BAR. Self-pride and the ego are the touchstone of most of these remarkable conversions." (Marshall, p. 76.)

Another passage from this book indicates the wider importance of this factor. Marshall writes that Field Marshal Sir Archibald Wavell once asked this question: "No man wants to die; what induces him to risk his life bravely?" The answer which comes out of Colonel Marshall's considerable experience and close observation is this: "The only answer which occurs to me as supportable in all that I have seen of man on the battlefield is that he will be persuaded largely by the same things which induce him to face life bravely—friendship, loyalty to responsibility, and knowledge that he is a repository of the faith and confidence of others." (*Ibid.*, pp. 160–161.)

Both interresponsibility and interdependence within the primary group are motivating forces of the first magnitude for the American soldier in combat. The political situation of his society and the ideology of his culture brings the individual into the formal Army structure. The formal structure prepares him for combat and takes him there. But the forces which actuate him for long periods while he is in combat are basically his loyalty to and his friendship with his buddies; in other words, his primary-group affiliations.

Negro Grouping /

So far our survey has shown
that the primary group is an important factor in the functioning of a unit and that in the stress of battle it is all the more important. Our next step is to indicate, by a study of Negro groupings in the armed services, that under certain conditions the patterns of primary-group cohesion prevail despite unusual contrary pulls, and under other circumstances they give way.

Briefly, the situation is this: When Negro troops are interspersed among white soldiers ("integrated" is the term commonly used) they become members of primary groups, and in combat the men of a primary group in an integrated unit are bound together as staunchly as in any other unit. But when present-day Negro troops are put into all-Negro units ("segregated"), the primary groups in the unit not infrequently break up in combat and each man seeks his safety alone and usually to the rear. Perhaps the main reason for this is that the fact of segregation increases the lack of confidence in each other as Negroes, a distrust which is held and implanted by potent sections of the larger society. And under battle stress, when the demand for mutual support is greatest, this undermining of confidence sometimes collapses the strength otherwise engendered in the primary group.

This is not a well-documented and fully validated conclusion. The evidence is fragmentary and mostly indirect; other factors, such as education, importantly affect the performance of Negro units. But this is an explanation which seems to fit the observed facts. And while the evidence is far from complete, it has been accrued by a kind of unwitting operational research. Because of various reasons of military expedience and nonmilitary pressure, Negroes have been utilized in the services in a variety of specific ways. Observations and analyses of the results of these different usages are not complete but they are nevertheless quite convincing. For they indicate that similar processes operated at every stage of the historical development of the subject. Thus, integrated units have consistently been successful from the point of view of the military command; yet, military commanders have regularly been averse to integration. In recent years the manifest military disadvantages of segregation have been among the factors which have brought about changes in policy. Our concern here is not with the ethics of military policy in this respect, but rather with the (often unforeseen) consequences of that policy at various times and circumstances.

NEGROES IN THE ARMY BEFORE WORLD WAR II

Even during the Revolutionary War, at the very outset of our national history, military commanders found the problem of Negro manpower a difficult one. Among the matters discussed by General George Washington with his chiefs of staff at a meeting on October 8, 1775, was the question of using Negroes in the Army. The decision was against their use and an order to that effect was issued on November 12, 1775. This decision was in accord with the recommendation of a civilian committee of the Continental Congress which had considered the matter earlier.

Within a few months this policy was reversed. By the time the order had been issued, Negroes were already serving creditably in the Continental Army, and General Washington found that it was neither militarily nor politically wise to expel them. Moreover, the British were energetically calling upon Negroes to rise up and join the king's colors, and the Americans could ill afford to alienate either slaves or freedmen. The upshot was that Negroes were not expelled from the Army or refused enlistment in it but, indeed, received with greater enthusiasm as the war went on. Most of the several thousand Negroes who served in the Revolutionary Army were scattered as individuals through the ranks, and after the war General Washington publicly stated that they had served well. (Reddick, pp. 12–15.)

During the Civil War, Union commanders grappled with the problem for two years before the decision was reached to admit Negroes into the ranks. Negroes were segregated, as they had not generally been before, into all-Negro units up to the size of the all-Negro XXV Corps. At this juncture in history, the important matter to many Negroes in the Union Army was that they had been given the right to fight as free men. That they were segregated was of little, if any, consequence to them then. This view was later to change. The right to fight became less of an invigorating force in itself, and the necessity of serving in segregated units became more of a detrimental factor. By the end of the Civil War, there were 178,985 Negroes in the Union Army. Only a very few were officers; most

Negro troops were infantrymen. They fought well in many engagements, white officers sought to be assigned to the command of Negro troops, and Negro soldiers received a number of resounding public commendations.

When the Army was reorganized in 1866 and put on a peacetime basis, six Negro regiments were established by law as a part of the Regular Army. At that period in history this move was not looked upon as a device for segregation but as a friendly and progressive step, as a recognition and reward for valor, so that thenceforward Negro soldiers would have an assured place in the American Army. (Reddick, pp. 16–18.)

The policy of segregating Negro soldiers was continued through World War I. While Negro supply and supporting units rendered good service, both at home and overseas, and some Negro combat units fought well, staff officers who studied the use of Negroes in World War I were far from satisfied that the best use had been made of Negro manpower in that conflict. The 1950 report of the President's Committee on Equality of Treatment and Opportunity in the Armed Services, appointed by President Truman and headed by Charles Fahy, makes a special note of these post-World War I studies: "... every study of Negro manpower utilization which was conducted by the Army War College between wars recommended that the Army never again form Negro units of divisional size. Despite these recommendations and contrary to the assurance which the Army gave to Selective Service that Negro divisions would not be formed, the 92d and 93d Divisions were reactivated in World War II." (President's Committee, p. 47.)

The Fahy Committee report also cites the testimony of an unnamed "distinguished general, a southerner," who in 1922 pointed out the relation of the primary group to race relations in the Army. This general warned that the employment of Negro troops in large separate units wasted manpower and fomented trouble. He declared that racial friction most frequently developed not between individuals but between groups, and he advised the Army to intersperse Negro soldiers one or two to a squad. Then "... the internal esprit which inevitably developed in a small group of men engaged in the same task would assure the Negro of acceptance and protect him against discrimination. The result would be more effective utilization of Negro manpower, less trouble, and better morale." (President's Committee, p. 49.)

This estimate concerning the way in which a Negro in a squad would come to share the esprit of the informal group and would be accepted as a member of the group has been exemplified recently in the Korean fighting and in garrison situations. And the general's judgment that the formation of large, all-Negro units tended to waste manpower and to aggravate rather than allay interracial tension was demonstrated again in World War II.

WORLD WAR II EXPERIENCE

The policy which the War Department was to follow through World War II was announced in a statement of October 9, 1940. It noted chiefly that the strength of Negro personnel in the Army would be maintained on the general basis of the proportion of the Negro population of the country and that "the policy of the War Department is not to intermingle colored and white enlisted personnel in the same regimental organizations. This policy has been proven satisfactory over a long period of years and to make changes would produce situations destructive to morale and detrimental to the preparations for national defense."

The Fahy Committee report dryly comments that, if military efficiency is taken as a criterion, the statement

that the Army's policy of segregation has proved satisfactory over a long period of years was not one which
could be documented by the files in the Army's Historical
Records Section or by the studies prepared by the Army
War College. "If the historical records established anything, they proved conclusively that the Army had not
received maximum efficient utilization from its segregated units and had experienced endless trouble. The War
College studies, while rarely recommending the abandonment of segregation, made the same conclusions in-
escapable." (President's Committee, p. 48.)

The military inefficiency promoted by Negro segregation in the Army during World War II was recognized by
the special board of general officers, headed by Lieutenant
General Gillem, which was appointed in 1945 to review
the facts concerning Negro manpower. Its report placed
a major responsibility for the shortcomings of Negro units
on the lack of adequate staff preparation and planning.
(Gillem Board report cited in Stouffer, I:586–587.)
However, it must be remembered that the staff officers
who should have made suitable preparation were confronted with a problem that not only affected but far trans-
cended the military bureaucracy. They, like General
George Washington and his staff before them, were aware
of strong and opposing forces in American life generally,
knowing that whatever decision they reached would be
open to violent criticism from civilian sources. They were
impaled on the horns of what Myrdal has called an
"American dilemma" and, thus impaled, staff officers in
any bureaucracy tend to become immobilized and to contribute little toward a solution of the problem.

As a result of this lack of adequate planning the policy
of Negro segregation was allowed to drift along during
the years of World War II, and Negro units were subjected to frequent reorganization, regrouping, and shifting from one type of training to another. Such mercurial

changes rarely enhance the efficiency of any unit; for Negro units there was the added and more serious encumbrance of segregation. Segregation entails a number of military disadvantages, such as the upgrading of some personnel beyond their real capacities and the disuse of the skills and abilities of other personnel. But the major disadvantage is the fact that being in an all-Negro unit steadily reminds the members of the unit of their disabilities as Negroes.

Many Negroes keenly resent their disadvantages and, not unnaturally, tend to see all their personal difficulties and any misfortune which befalls them as being caused by racial discrimination. This racial perspective becomes all the more fixed and baleful among the members of an all-Negro unit. And the resentment cannot easily be dissipated or deflected but levies a steady toll on the efficiency of such a unit.

The prevalence of this racial perspective among Negro troops in World War II is shown in studies made by the Research Branch analysts. They note that many complaints common to soldiers of both races acquired a special significance among Negro soldiers by being invested with the quality of racial discrimination. "Thus it became not merely a matter of lack of recreation facilities, poor food, slowness of promotions, and so on—all such specific points of dissatisfaction took on the potentiality of being regarded as instances of discrimination against Negroes." (Stouffer, I:502.)

One outcome of the racial perspective was that Negroes, on the average, tended to show less enthusiasm for the war than did whites, and manifested somewhat greater reluctance to go overseas or to enter combat. Be it noted that the existence of all-Negro units did not cause this racial perspective, but Army segregation did enhance its ill effects on military efficiency. Many Negro individuals and Negro units performed ably and efficiently overseas as well as at home, both in garrison and in combat. But the over-all performance of Negro manpower was very probably less efficient than it would have been without segregation.

It may well be that a process applies here which has also been observed in group relations in industrial plants. A group which is stigmatized as inferior, and does not accept this judgment, lowers its output and does other things to antagonize the group which considers itself superior. Although, in doing so, they further lower their rank in the eyes of the superior group, they have the satisfaction of getting back at the superiors by being inefficient. This further stimulates the antagonism between the groups. (Homans, 1950, pp. 297–298.)

Segregation in the Army was also one of the factors which tended to make Negro troops less sure than they otherwise would have been about their personal commitment to the war. "Negroes, dissatisfied with the prevailing system of race relations and their inferior status, were less likely than whites to accept official formulations of war aims and view the war as of central concern to them. For Negroes there were two struggles—the war which preoccupied the nation and their own endeavor to achieve higher status in that nation." Moreover, the Research Branch analysts go on to say, individual failure among Negroes was in general less stigmatized—in the Negro group because it often seemed to be less a function of the individual's qualities than of disadvantages based on treatment of his race, and in the white group because whites assumed that the Negro was inferior and expected less from him. (Stouffer, I:525–526.)

Segregation did nothing to raise the low opinion of Negro abilities held by some whites, but tended to confirm it. Negro units, by the very fact that they were segregated, tended to be less efficient than a comparable white unit which did not operate under the disadvantages of segregation. This lesser efficiency was taken as proof of Negro inferiority, and Negro inferiority was cited as one justification for segregation in the Army. When a low valuation is put on Negro or any other kind of manpower, it is hardly surprising that the returns from the use of that manpower will also be low. This cycle has been termed by Merton "the self-fulfilling prophecy." (Merton, p. 185.)

This circular process was especially damaging to efficiency in leadership. We have noted above that good officers are an essential factor in good unit performance, and that an officer, in order to be an effective leader, must set up bonds of identification between himself and the enlisted men. While World War II Negro troops in overwhelming majority preferred Negro officers to white officers, their officers, with a few exceptions, were white. (Stouffer, I:585.) White officers generally resented being assigned to Negro units; their resentment was communicated to the enlisted men under their command. The Negro enlisted men, already specially sensitive because of their racial perspective to white antagonism both real and imagined, reciprocally resented their officers. Under such conditions, it was not easy to establish identification between unit officers and men. Leadership in Negro units was frequently comparatively poor, and, with ineffective officers, the performance of the all-Negro unit was often below its potential under more favorable circumstances.

The nature of leadership in a Negro outfit is described in an account of the Second Cavalry Division written by a sociologist, Arnold M. Rose. He observes that this division was given poor training and had officers of less than average ability. Since many of the officers believed that Negroes could not make combat troops, training was loose and combat discipline lax. Then every failure in training was taken as proof that it was impossible to train Negro soldiers for combat.

Other factors also brought about the low morale in the

Second Cavalry Division. There were numerous "incidents" which proved to the men that their officers had little regard for them. Stories were told of how white officers insulted the few Negro officers in the division. The division refused to take jurisdiction over a case in which a Negro soldier got in trouble with a local Southern civilian authority. "Remarks passing between white officers about the character and quality of their men were overheard by some of the enlisted men. The lack of respect of the officers for their men engendered lack of respect of the men for their officers." Rose quotes one Negro sergeant as saying, "We spend too much time in hating and fighting our officers to have much energy left for the Germans." This may not have been a typical comment, but a study of the division made it clear that the morale of the men, however morale was defined and measured, was lower among Second Cavalry men than among other troops. (Rose, 1947, pp. 27–29.)

Similar observations have been made by an anthropologist, E. T. Hall, Jr., who served as an officer in a Negro unit for two and one half years. He writes that white officers generally did not desire service with Negro troops. Whenever he and his fellow officers who had command of Negro troops would go to a larger headquarters, they would be greeted by the phrase, "Boy, am I glad I don't have them" or some similar remark. There was a consistent rumor that after eighteen months with Negro troops, an officer could get a transfer to a white unit.

Dr. Hall tells of the visit of an officer from the Inspector General's Department to the unit. In the course of the inspection, the visitor asked the officers when they were going to ask him the question. When they did not know just what question he meant, "he explained that whenever he inspected a colored unit, the officers always got him in a corner and asked him how to get out." A few white officers actually preferred service with Negro troops, and these officers almost without exception had superior companies. With proper leadership, Hall observed, Negro units could and did perform superbly well, and situations which might have boiled up interracial tensions could be avoided. Thus special plans were made for a forty-day sea voyage on a troop transport with both Negro and white units aboard. Although the voyage was trying, the plans worked well and there were no racial conflicts among the men. (Hall, pp. 404–405, 408.)

Such instances demonstrated that with adequate planning and leadership some of the trouble between racial groups in the Army could be averted and the performance of Negro units stepped up in efficiency. But the fact of segregation tended to make for inadequate planning and ineffective leadership in Negro units.

The exact cost of segregation in World War II is not measureable. The waste of maintaining two sets of units in every branch of the service between which no exchange of personnel is permissible is pointed out by Charles Dollard and Donald Young. They also note that segregation involved both the overbuilding and underuse of facilities. Thus Fort Huachuca, the only large, all-Negro camp in the country, was used to capacity for only a part of the war, yet its hospital and other overhead services had to be maintained continuously. In other camps, recreational facilities were duplicated without either of the duplicates being put to full use. Another aspect of the waste in segregation was the commissioning of some Negroes who would not have qualified as officers in a free-for-all competition. And at the same time other Negroes, qualified in specialties in which no Negro units had been organized, were not used effectively.

"But the least measureable and the most serious cost of all was the decreased efficiency of Negro units. The constant reminder of their second-class citizenship which the whole business of segregation involved is deadening to the spirit and to initiative. The full measure of this cost may be found in the unhappy history of the 92d Division." This division, the authors note, had a very uneven combat record in Italy. A study of its performance and of the underlying reasons for its shortcomings was made by Truman Gibson, a Negro lawyer, who was then assistant secretary of war. "Lack of sufficient preparation and of well trained leadership, the discouragements of Jim Crow in military service and in civilian life" were among the causes for poor morale and performance which Gibson pointed to in his report.

The loss of the potential usefulness of this division and of the other Negro divisions was only a part, and perhaps only a small part, of the total military cost of segregation. Dollard and Young are careful to point out that against these costs must be balanced some savings. They note that any sudden move away from the principal of segregation probably would have brought reprisals from Southern Congressmen and also would have diverted an undue amount of the time of the War Department over this issue. From the standpoint of individual Negroes, segregation plus the Army policy of having at least token representation of Negroes in all branches of service meant that some Negroes were offered valuable training opportunities which otherwise would have been closed to them. Finally, Dollard and Young note, some Negroes who were accustomed to the pattern of segregation as civilians, expressed a preference for continued segregation in the Army because they feared the consequences of nonsegregation. As we shall see below, the experience of the postwar years in the integration of Negroes and whites in Army units, reveals that all these supposed savings are very dubious ones.

After listing the presumed advantages of segregation, Dollard and Young note that the disadvantages were very great: "The army complained with some truth that Negro soldiers would not follow Negro officers in combat. Yet such a lack of confidence merely reflected the fact that, implicit in the army's own practices, was the judgment that Negro and white officers are different species. What could be more blind than the policy which expects men to risk death behind an officer who from the start is labeled inferior? How can we ever expect Negroes to recognize leadership in their own ranks so long as that recognition is withheld by the white majority?" (Dollard and Young, pp. 68, 111–114.)

There was another kind of segregation in the Army which did not have the same consequences as did the segregation of Negroes. This was the formation of units composed of Nisei, Japanese-Americans. The difference between the all-Nisei units and the all-Negro units was discussed in the testimony of a former Nisei officer before the Fahy Committee. "The Nisei fought as well as they did, he [Mike Matsuoka] said, not to justify segregation but to discredit it and demonstrate their right to be treated as full citizens. Furthermore, the Nisei outfit in Italy was specially selected, with a GCT [General Classification Test] spread far above that of the average white unit." (Kenworthy, p. 30.)

The latter factor, the selected quality of the men in all-Nisei units, was important. But the former factor is the more important. To these Nisei soldiers, segregation in the Army meant a chance to prove that they were as good soldiers and citizens as anyone else—or better. To most Negroes, Army segregation was just a familiar carry-over of the galling civilian pattern. And in their view there was little chance of proving themselves— no matter how good their performance might be—so long as the segregation pattern was maintained. The Nisei, as had many Negro soldiers in the Civil War, perceived segregation as a challenge which they could and did meet. Negro troops in World War II more typically perceived segregation not as a challenge for personal achievement but as an assurance of personal defeat.

Whatever estimate is made of the military costs of Negro segregation, the evidence indicates that these were not entirely necessary. In the first place, Negro soldiers had about the same attitudes and behavior patterns as did white soldiers except, as discussed above, in matters which related to race problems. To be sure, the Research Branch surveys did show some differences in attitude between Negro and white troops—while Negroes had lower motivation for overseas duty or for combat (partly because of their racial perspective), they also had greater pride in outfit, higher sense of importance of their army jobs, and greater interest in their jobs. But in general the attitudes and behavior patterns of the Negro soldier were very much the same as that of the white soldier. (Stouffer, I:488–489, 524, 526, 535.)

Hence any arguments for segregation on the grounds that Negroes have a basically different culture and so do not share the way of life and the values of white society in general were demonstrably invalid by the data of the Research Branch surveys as well as by a wealth of other evidence.

Second, many Negroes were qualified by ability and education to serve in posts of greater responsibility than those to which they were restricted by the policy of segregation. Negroes who had the qualifications to become officers had much less chance of doing so than did whites of equal educational and ability levels. (Stouffer, I:489–502.) Segregation could not rationally be justified on the grounds that Negroes could satisfactorily perform only unskilled tasks.

Finally, in those cases during World War II where segregation was modified or abolished, the results were favorable from the military point of view. Thus any misgivings which may have been entertained about the complete integration of Negro and white personnel in officer-candidate schools were demonstrated to be groundless. There were in all about a score of integrated schools, each producing specialists for some one branch of service. Whites and Negroes slept, ate, and trained together with a minimum of friction and with no incidents worthy of record. (Dollard and Young, p. 68.)

Another important experiment in the modification of segregation was tried in the European theater toward the end of the war. The need for infantry replacements was so great that it was decided to accept Negro volunteers and organize them as separate platoons within white infantry companies with white officers and white noncoms. An order was issued by Lieutenant General John C. H. Lee, on December 26, 1944, permitting Negro enlisted men in service units within his command to volunteer for duty as infantrymen. All such volunteers had to sacrifice any ratings they held; about twenty-five hundred took advantage of the opportunity and eventually served in combat. They were placed in eleven different divisions.

Shortly after V-E Day, the Research Branch conducted an extensive survey in seven of these eleven divisions in order to evaluate how this program had worked out. The results were clear cut. In the companies in which Negro platoons had served, the vast majority of white officers and white enlisted men gave approval of their perform-ance in combat. In response to the question, "How well did the colored soldiers in this company perform in com-bat?" 84 per cent of the officers and 81 per cent of the enlisted men said, "Very well"; 16 per cent of the officers and 17 per cent of the enlisted men replied, "Fairly well"; none of the officers and 1 per cent of the enlisted men answered, "Not so well"; and not even 1 per cent of either the officers or the enlisted men answered, "Not well at all." Moreover, there was some indication in the data that the performance of Negro troops was rated highest by the officers and men in the companies in which the colored platoons had had the most severe fighting. (Stouffer, I:587–589.)

The Research Branch survey showed that relationships between Negro and white infantrymen turned out to be far better than their officers had expected: 96 per cent of the officers questioned on this point reported themselves agreeably surprised. And the more intimately the men had participated in a mixed-company organization of Negroes and whites, the less opposition there was to it. Men who actually were in a company containing a Negro platoon were most favorable toward the mixed-company idea, men in larger units in which there were no mixed companies were least favorable, while men in all-white companies within a regiment or division containing mixed companies held intermediate opinions.

An especially significant piece of evidence is that about two-thirds of the men in an average white company said that they disliked the idea of mixed companies very much *before* a Negro platoon was introduced to their company. After having been in a mixed company, the proportion of men who said they disliked mixed companies very much fell to 7 per cent. From this, the Research Branch writers comment, "we can get some conception of the revolution in attitudes that took place among these men as a result of enforced contacts." (Stouffer, I:593–595.)

The last-mentioned set of statistics not only shows that white troops can be agreeably surprised by the modification of segregation, but also demonstrates the differences between a verbal response to a hypothetical situation and actual behavior in a real situation. Since two-thirds of the whites said that they would dislike mixed companies very much, it might have been assumed that mixed-company organization would not work out—that great friction might develop among the platoons of the company and combat efficiency would suffer. No such outcome resulted, however likely it may have seemed from a naïve interpretation of the questionnaire results. This, in turn, cast doubt on another of the principal justifications for segregation. The premise is stated in War Department Pamphlet 20–6, 1944, *Command of Negro Troops,* as follows: "It is important to understand that separate organization is a matter of practical military expediency and not an endorsement of belief in racial distinction . . . A 1943 survey of attitudes of white and colored soldiers indicates that the odds are very much in favor of less interracial friction if colored and white enlisted men continue to be organized in separate racial units." (Cited in U. S. War Department, *Army Talk,* p. 3.)

While the 1943 survey conducted by the Research Branch showed that 84 per cent of white soldiers who were questioned thought that Negroes and whites should be in separate outfits, it did not mean that the men of this 84 per cent had considered the military cost of segregation; nor that these men would never tolerate the abolition of segregation; nor did it portend that carefully planned integration would not work. As we shall see by the record of the postwar years, the "revolution of attitude" among white troops who serve in fully integrated units is probably as great as the earlier change of attitude among soldiers who had seen combat in a mixed company and had reversed their previously unfavorable opinion of mixed units.

The same process occurs in industry. E. C. Hughes comments that the polling of white workers to find whether they favor the hiring of Negroes as fellow workers would almost anywhere ·result in an emphatic, "No." "But Negroes have been successfully employed among white workers. . . Polling attitudes, on this simple basis, gives little clue to the probable behavior of the old workers to the new." Hughes also notes that it does not therefore follow that racial preferences and dislikes have no bearing on the way the races will work together. For racial attitudes themselves take on new dimensions when looked at in the framework of the human relations prevailing in industry. In one industrial situation observed by Hughes, in which Negro and white girls worked at individual polishing tasks in the same room, none of the Negro girls was part of the informal group in which some of the white girls participated. This was probably because the management impressed on the Negro worker that she had to prove herself and so she felt that she had to be a "solitary" in order to produce enough to keep her job. In this situation, integration was successful enough in that no strong desires for segregation were evident. But the social influence of race was not wiped out by integration. (Hughes, pp. 512, 519.)

In the Army also, the success of the modification of segregation during World War II did not mean that racial attitudes were of no consequence. It did mean that the consequences of experiments with race contacts had to be considered in relation to other social factors and especially the force of the primary group. And the specific experiments of World War II were comparatively limited. In the officer-candidate schools, the number of Negroes was small and both the Negroes and whites were specially selected and trained. In the mixed-company operations, the men in the Negro platoons were volunteers. There was still segregation within platoons, and special precautions were taken to ensure the smooth functioning of the mixed companies. Moreover, the situation was one of predominantly victorious combat—a context particularly favorable to harmonious relations within a unit.

All these considerations were stated by the men themselves on the questionnaires returned by the white officers and enlisted men who had participated in mixed companies. Many took occasion to note that relationships were better in combat than in the garrison. Relationships in combat could be regarded as working relationships rather than social relationships. They could be confined more narrowly to a functionally specific basis than could contacts involved in community living. "Far from being a 'test case' in ordinary Negro-white relations, the combat setting may be regarded as a special case making for good relationships, for the sense of common danger and common obligation was high, the need for unity was at a maximum and there was great consciousness of shared experience of an intensely emotional kind." (Stouffer, I:592–593.)

These experiments, then, demonstrated that under certain conditions segregation could be modified with no ensuing friction and with a considerable gain in military efficiency. Just how greatly segregation could be modified beyond these conditions remained to be shown by the experience of other services than the Army, and by experience within the Army between 1945 and 1951. To that part of the record we now proceed.

THE NAVY: FROM EXCLUSION TO INTEGRATION

Since 1942 Navy policy concerning Negroes has changed from exclusion (except for mess attendant) to segregation and then to integration. The results of integration are reported as being uniformly satisfactory. No shipboard friction along racial lines has developed as some had feared; both Negro and white sailors seem well enough content with the arrangement; and no shattering complaints from civilian sources on this score have so far affected either the efficiency of or the appropriations for the Navy.

One observer, writing in 1947, tells of his visit aboard a battleship. In the crew were about a hundred Negroes, half of them in general service, as well as a Negro midshipman from Annapolis on a training cruise. "There was no sign of racial strain—in fact, the situation had been produced so quietly as a natural development of Navy policy that the public was unaware of the changes and the men themselves were unconscious of the fact that they were making modern history." (Granger, p. 68.)

The present policy of integration actually marks a return to the earlier Navy policy. The Navy had enlisted Negroes for general service from the earliest period of United States history until the end of World War I, and Negro sailors had served well throughout the naval establishment. It was only after World War I that the enlistment of Negroes was stopped and, when it was opened again in 1932, Negroes could only be recruited in the messman's branch.

This practice continued until 1942 when the Navy announced that Negroes would be enlisted for general service as well as for mess attendants. The Negroes thus accepted for general service were trained in segregated camps and schools, utilized in segregated units, and limited in assignment to shore installations and harbor craft. But as the number of Negroes assigned to the Navy by Selective Service grew, employment could not be found for all of them in shore installations and on harbor craft. It was soon realized that many Negro recruits possessed technical skills which could not be put to use so long as Navy policy prevented the assignment of Negroes to sea-going vessels.

After considerable staff discussion and some tentative experiments, a decisive experiment was tried. In August, 1944, Negroes were assigned to twenty-five auxiliary ships of the fleet. Not more than 10 per cent of the enlisted personnel aboard any ship were Negroes, but these Negroes were integrated completely with white crews. From this experiment it was learned that Negroes could be placed in white crews without trouble. And in April, 1945, it was announced that Negro personnel would thenceforth be eligible for service in all auxiliary fleet vessels, though the 10 per cent quota for each ship would still be observed. By July, 1945, all segregated schools and camps were abolished. These modifications of segregation worked so well that the Navy abolished segregation entirely in February, 1946, and general service assignments have since been open to Negroes without restriction. (Nelson, 183–205.)

When the Fahy Committee made its thorough investigation in 1949–1950, it found that the new Navy directive had worked eminently well. The committee interviewed officers and enlisted men, both white and Negro; all those questioned said that there had been no racial friction rising out of integration. This evidence, the committee's report notes, serves to confirm the idea that respect created between individuals through competence on the job—the value which the workman sets upon workmanship—would translate itself over a period of time into personal respect and would facilitate the accommodation of the two races in their daily life, and thus act to break down artificial barriers. This process has been discussed above as an aspect of the integrating power of the primary group in a military unit.

The committee's report notes that in its about-face of policy the Navy had been chiefly influenced by considerations of military efficiency and the need to economize human resources. The findings on the results of the policy of integration in the Navy are summarized in the following words:

"The Navy had defended the nonutilization of Negroes in general service by citing the lower level of Negro skills and by appealing to the necessity of maintaining ship efficiency and ship morale. It had discovered that, as individuals, Negroes could be trained and utilized in as wide a range of skills as whites, and that failure to use them as individuals resulted in a waste of manpower which neither the Navy nor the country could afford. Still driven by the imperative need for skilled men, the Navy had put Negro ratings aboard ship and found that no trouble resulted. In defense of its new policy the Navy now cites the skills of its Negro manpower and ship efficiency." (President's Committee, p. 24.)

THE AIR FORCE: TOWARD THE ABANDONMENT
OF SEGREGATION

Some military officials maintained that the happy experience of the Navy with integration was not necessarily applicable to the Army and Air Force because in the Navy only small numbers of Negroes were involved whereas in the other services Negroes comprised 7 to 10 per cent of the total enlisted personnel. The recent record of the Air Force offers evidence that integration yields similarly satisfactory results even where larger numbers of Negroes are involved.

At the end of World War II the Air Force maintained the same policy on Negro manpower as the Army. Negro enlisted strength was restricted to 10 per cent, Negroes were utilized mainly in segregated units, and job opportunities for Negroes were greatly limited. Save for three all-Negro units—a fighter squadron, a fighter group, and a bombardment group—Negroes in the Air Force were used chiefly in service capacities and for heavy-duty work regardless of their individual skills and aptitudes. The great waste of this policy in the Army Air Corps was accurately predicted in a memorandum written early in 1941 by William H. Hastie, a Negro attorney and now a federal judge, who was then civilian aide to the secretary of war. Despite Hastie's well-considered—and as it turned out, prophetic—study, Air Corps planners made a series of inadequate compromises on the problem which intensified the waste. (Hastie, pp. 5 ff.)

In 1946 and 1947 a series of staff memoranda prepared in the Air Force pointed out that the established policy of segregation condemned men of superior skill to jobs where their abilities were wasted. It also forced the employment of men with lower skills in positions for which they were not equipped. Recommendations were made in these memoranda that Negroes in the Air Force be used only on the basis of their individual qualifications and that no job in the Air Force should carry a color bar. (President's Committee, pp. 34–35.)

However, these memoranda also recommended that segregation had to be maintained because of social custom and because of the possibility of difficulties between Negro and white airmen if they were placed in the same unit. In these latter recommendations the staff officers were dealing with social rather than purely military matters. As it turned out, they were as wrong in their judgments of the social situation as they were right in their appraisal of the military situation which maintained that there should be no race distinction made on the Air Force job.

In June, 1949, after a good deal of discussion within the Air Force staff and between the top Air Force officials and the secretary of defense, a new program for Negro manpower was instituted. It abolished enlistment quotas, job restrictions, and much of the segregation for Negroes, but did allow for the continued existence of some all-Negro units. But the three all-Negro combat units were disbanded and their personnel reassigned.

After the program had been in operation for six months, the staff of the Fahy Committee investigated seven major Air Force bases. It was found that complete integration had been reached as far as military duties were concerned and only one base still had a segregated unit.

In discussing the new program with commanding officers, the committee's staff brought forth significant evidence. These commanders, almost without exception, stated that they had put the new policy into effect with some misgivings. They had not questioned the fact that segregation constituted waste but they had doubted whether many Negroes would be able to qualify for technical positions in open competition with whites. In the words of the President's Committee: "They [had] questioned whether the gain in manpower utilization would be worth the trouble they expected from assigning Negroes to white units. Without exception commanding officers reported that their fears had not been borne out by events." Many more Negroes than the commanders had expected had demonstrated a capacity to compete on an equal basis, to absorb technical training successfully, and to perform ably in technical assignments. And the troubles they had feared had never materialized.

"Furthermore, commanders testified that racial incidents had diminished, rather than increased, since the new policy had gone into effect. With all schools and jobs open on a basis of merit, officers were no longer plagued with complaints of discrimination. Some officers who candidly stated their personal preference for the old ways nevertheless volunteered that the new program benefited the service and caused less trouble." (President's Committee, pp. 41–42.)

At the time the Fahy Committee was making these studies in January, 1950, about three-fourths of the Negroes in the Air Force performed their military duties side by side with white airmen. The presumably touchy matter of recreational facilities was left largely to the discretion of the individual commanding officer. The disposition of the commanding officers was to allow relationships to evolve according to the wishes of the men. And this led to a trend in the direction of shared facilities. There has since been an accelerating trend in the direction of complete integration in the Air Force both in regard to military duties and social and recreational facilities. This trend, far from bringing about any accentuation of interracial tension, has apparently diminished the incidence and the intensity of friction.

THE ARMY: TOWARD MODIFICATION OF SEGREGATION

In the Army, as in the Air Force, it was realized after World War II that the methods of utilizing Negro manpower had not been satisfactory and that in the postwar Army some changes were in order. As previously noted, a special board of general officers, under the chairmanship of Lieutenant General Alvan C. Gillem, was set up by the Army in October, 1945, and was charged with submitting recommendations to the secretary of war and the chief of staff.

The Gillem Board found that many Negroes in the Army were indeed qualified by education and skill for positions of greater responsibility and variety than were open to them under the then established policy. But the best means of using these abilities, the board believed, was by increasing the number and kind of all-Negro units, and by using individual Negroes in overhead (mainly housekeeping) installations, rather than by discarding quotas and opening all Army opportunities to qualified Negroes. The eighteen specific recommendations made by the Gillem Board to implement the broader use of Negro manpower need not be discussed in detail here. They were published in War Department Circular 124, 27 April 1946, and have been the subject of numerous memoranda, articles, and comments. The important consideration for our purposes is that the War Department put many Gillem Board recommendations into effect. The War Department attempted to equalize the job opportunities of white and

Negro soldiers by creating new Negro units and by opening up overhead installations to Negroes. But the principle of segregation was largely upheld, with only minor modifications.

On examining the results of these measures three years after they had been put into effect, the Fahy Committee found that they had generally failed to accomplish the broad objectives of the new program as stated by the Gillem Board. The committee's report observes that even the modified form of segregation was conducive to inefficiency in two ways. "By requiring skilled Negroes to serve in racial units, the army lost skills which could find no place in Negro organizations. On the other hand, by concentrating large numbers of unskilled Negroes in combat units, it multiplied inefficiency." (President's Committee, p. 55.)

The measures recommended by the Gillem Board to remedy this situation had not done so to any appreciable degree. In the three years nineteen units had been converted from white to Negro designation. This somewhat increased the number of jobs available to Negroes but, since the units were of a type in which Negroes had already been serving, it did not do much to expand the types of jobs available. The experimental grouping of Negro and white units in composite organizations, as recommended by the Gillem Board, had been done in a manner which was not very fruitful. Some Negro battalions had been assigned to white regiments, and there were some instances of Negro companies serving in white battalions. But the adverse effects of segregation apply in an all-Negro company as well as in a Negro division, so these relatively feeble experiments could hardly improve anything.

The use of Negroes in overhead units had also somewhat increased the range of jobs available to Negroes but there were still many jobs which were unattainable for them. In many specialties for which qualified Negroes were available but for which they could not apply, the Army was seriously under strength. In all, the previous waste of manpower had not been much reduced under the Gillem Board program. Negro units still did not offer as wide a range of jobs as were available in white units. Therefore Negroes were often not given the MOS (military-occupation specialty) classification for which they were qualified. Hence they could not receive school training for improvement in the specialties for which they already had some training.

The two principal conclusions drawn by the Fahy Committee from a review of the three years of the Gillem Board program were: "First, the individual skilled Negro was not getting equal opportunity at Army jobs and Army schools; second, he was unlikely to get it while the army limited his assignment to Negro and overhead units and could refuse him enlistment under the quota system." (President's Committee, p. 60.)

The failure of the Gillem Board program had been foretold soon after it was announced. Thus Rose, writing in 1947, stated that because the Gillem Board recommended the continuance of segregation, even though all-Negro divisions were abolished, ". . . there is little doubt that the policy which wrecked the Second Cavalry Division, and made the 92d and 93d Infantry Divisions inefficient, will continue in the Army. It may therefore be concluded that Army policy on the utilization of Negro troops is a failure. The Negro problem in the Army—which is simply a problem of getting efficient action for money and effort spent in maintaining and training men—remains." (Rose, 1947, p. 30.)

The self-aggravating and self-defeating cycle of the segregation policy had not been broken as it had been in the Navy. A simplified formulation of this cycle is: Segregation makes for increased consciousness of their racial status among Negroes; this consciousness leads to greater sensitivity by Negroes to slights, real or imagined, from whites; this sensitivity creates difficulties for the officers of Negro units—officers who are generally none too secure in their role as officers and in their assignment to a Negro unit; this brings about greater discord than usually exists between the officers and the enlisted men; this discord makes for the lower military efficiency of Negro units; and that low efficiency bolsters the concept of the shiftless Negro fostered by some whites—which is one of the justifications propounded for the continued enforcement of segregation.

This cycle is self-defeating because segregation does not accomplish the expedient, short-range goal of decreasing racial friction which it is supposed to achieve. Instead it frequently tends to increase such friction. And it is self-aggravating because commanding officers frequently respond to the troubles intensified by segregation by increasing the restrictions of segregation.

The Fahy Committee investigation led to a revision of Army procedure. In January, 1950, a new policy was published in Special Regulations 600–629–1. Under its terms the color bar was removed from all Army jobs and schools, all racial quotas were abolished including the former 10 per cent limit, and a Negro could now be assigned to any unit in the Army as his qualifications merit and as military considerations indicate. Segregated units were still maintained but would presumably decline in number and strength since a Negro no longer had to serve in a segregated unit only. The committee recognized that since all-Negro units were already attached or assigned to larger organizations which formed a part of the "immediate striking force," the problem of total abolition of segregation was more complicated in the Army than in the other services. On these grounds the committee did not press for complete integration and was satisfied that the new policy of January, 1950, was an effective step forward in the more efficient use of Negro manpower in the Army.

The first reports on the effects of the Army's new policy were entirely consistent with the evidence of earlier experience. Where segregation had been abolished, under carefully planned conditions, the Army has benefited by increased manpower efficiency and decreased racial conflict. Where segregation had been retained, complaints of discrimination continued to well up and interracial hostility sporadically broke out.

These reports are not complete or authoritative. They are mainly from journalistic sources and not based on long or extensive investigations. But they are congruent with the findings of such thorough studies as those conducted by the Research Branch.

Thus a Negro newspaperman, Collins C. George, made a tour of Army and Air Force installations in 1951. His articles, published in the *Pittsburgh Courier,* reflect an understandable tendency to see good in integration and bad in segregation, but the factual evidence he presents appears reliable. In the *Courier* of April 21, 1951 (pp. 1, 10), he describes his observations at Fort Jackson, South Carolina. Two divisions are in training there of which one, the Eighth (Golden Arrow) Division, is completely integrated. In this division a large proportion of the men, both white and Negro, are from the South. Whites and Negroes have the same barracks, the same mess; they work, study, and play side by side. Not only is there an absolute minimum of racial friction but, George notes with some surprise, some white soldiers whose speech indicates that they are from the deep South are becoming close buddies with Negro soldiers. "It seems that once the shock of the new experience wears off it is the southern white soldier who forms the warmest and closest personal friendships with the Negro GI." One all-Negro unit is still maintained at Fort Jackson in the headquarters of the post complement. Of this unit George writes: "Just as in any segregated outfit, grievances fancied or real, become magnified and all is placed on a racial basis and just about all the stories of racial bias in the handling of men stemmed direct from the all-colored Section 2 of the Post headquarters unit."

While one of the two divisions at this camp is completely integrated, the other, the Thirty-first (Dixie) Division, is not, and this, writes George, brings about a strange situation of segregation in reverse. The Thirty-first Division is a National Guard unit from Mississippi and Alabama. Since the general facilities of the post are open to Negroes, the Dixie Division and its facilities have to be isolated from the others. And they are isolated in what used to be the colored area of the camp.

At other Army installations in the South, as at Camp Gordon, Georgia, integration has been similarly successful on the job and in the schools, but has not been fully carried out in social and recreational matters because of civilian attitudes. However, in the *Pittsburgh Courier* of April 28, 1951 (p. 1), George reports two small but significant episodes which may portend future trends. A Negro second lieutenant was stationed as an instructor in one of the service schools in Camp Gordon. When the officers of his school complement sought to have a dance on the post, they found that no white girls from near-by Augusta would attend if the Negro lieutenant were present. The dance was held and he stayed away. But a good many of his white colleagues stayed away also rather than attend an affair from which a fellow officer was barred. Similarly, there was a Negro major among the students at another service school at Camp Gordon. When his fellow officers were refused permission to have a dance in the town if the major were present, the officers decided to hold their affair on the post where the Army, not the civilian, custom prevailed. Presumably this dance could be held without the presence of townspeople.

Trivial as these incidents are in themselves, they may indicate an important process. It can be stated in this way: When a Negro operates and is accepted as part of the primary group within a military unit, then an affront to him as a Negro is considered an affront to the group, and the other members will protect their colleague. Under such circumstances, neither the Negroes or the whites of the unit are likely to encourage racial tension either within the unit or outside it.

All service clubs for enlisted men at Camp Gordon are open to Negroes. In only one of them, however, are Negro hostesses stationed, and to this center, naturally enough, most Negro enlisted men come. Even this minor kind of segregation in social facilities is considered undesirable by some commanding officers (as at Fort Dix, New Jersey), who obviate this situation by placing a Negro and a white hostess together in the same club.

A good deal of success of the integration program, according to George and other commentators, depends on the inclination and tact of the commanding officer. The smooth progress of the integration program at Fort Jackson, South Carolina, was attributed in no small part to the ability of the commanding general. Similarly at Fort Dix, New Jersey, where a program of integration has been in effect since January, 1951, the efforts of the commanding general are given full credit by George (*Pittsburgh Courier*, April 21, 1951, p. 1; May 5, 1951, p. 1). At Fort Dix, indeed, the integration extends both to officers and enlisted men, on military duty and off the job. Thus a Negro captain is in command of an integrated company, and mixed dances are held. The Negro newspaperman writes that "almost no fault can now be found in the racial policies of the post."

Whatever appraisal may be appropriate when better evidence is available, these reports show that the Army's experience with a program of integration has been broadly the same as the Navy's. Few difficulties are encountered in having Negroes and whites work side by side in the performance of military duties. Social and recreation integration is more complicated, partly because of civilian influences, but no outraged outcry has arisen from Southern white civilians in the neighborhood of Army posts where integration has been effected.

In 1950–1951 both integration and segregation in combat as well as in garrison were tested. Again the reports are fragmentary but again they point to clear and consistent conclusions. In combat, integration is militarily more efficient than segregation. Expert testimony on this matter comes from Colonel S. L. A. Marshall, who was placed on temporary active duty in 1950 to study at first hand the effectiveness of U. S. Army tactics in Korea. In an interview reported in the *New York Times* of December 17, 1950 (p. 13), Marshall said that a special study was made of companies in the Second Division in which whites and Negroes were mixed, i.e., integrated. "In my judgment those companies handled themselves as efficiently and courageously as any companies in the war. In fact, the mixed Company B of the 9th Infantry Regiment gave the bravest account of itself of any company." When Company B's white commander was wounded in the first hour of battle in the Kunu operation, where the Second Division covered the Eighth Army's retreat before the big Chinese Communist offensive, a Negro first lieutenant took over command for the rest of the battle. He served with great distinction, Marshall notes.

One *New York Times* war correspondent with the

Eighth Army in Korea begins his report in the issue of February 9, 1951 (p. 3), as follows: "U. S. Army Infantry outfits that are discarding Negro segregation practices in Korea are discovering that removal of the color line among fighting troops is paying good dividends both in morale and in battle." The evidence for this statement came from the reporter's observation that in some units in Korea, white replacements are being assigned to Negro units and Negro replacements to white units. This usually occurred because local commanders had to take whatever replacements they could get without delay to bring their units back to fighting strength. And the commanders found that this practice had a beneficial rather than a detrimental effect on the effectiveness of their units. As the replacements intermingled more and more within the outfit, friendships were formed which were in no wise hampered by the soldier's color. There had been instances of Negro officers having command of white troops and of Negro officers outranking white officers without any special friction in either case.

The correspondent cites an interview with a white lieutenant who said that when he was assigned to work with Negroes and whites together, he told his superiors that although he was a deeply indoctrinated Southerner he would try his best to go halfway and even more. Actually he found he had never had to go more than halfway. Usually he was not conscious of making any special effort at all. This interview indicates again that, once the color barrier is removed by order, a white soldier from the South generally finds few difficulties in working and fighting side by side with a Negro soldier—in accepting him as a fellow member of the primary group.

Similar conclusions were drawn by H. H. Martin, a correspondent whose article on the performance of Negro troops in Korea appeared in the *Saturday Evening Post* of June 16, 1951. At the time that article was written, some 25 per cent of the Negro infantry replacements in the Korean theater were assigned as individuals scattered throughout the Command and not to all-Negro units. At the same time, the all-Negro 24th Infantry Regiment and other segregated units were in the line. Thus, perhaps more by accident than design, there was at least an approach to controlled experiments on the combat performance of Negro soldiers in segregated and nonsegregated units.

The integration here was more thoroughgoing than in the World War II experiment in which Negro soldiers in line companies were still put in separate platoons. But the results, Martin writes, were generally the same: Officers commanding integrated units reported that Negro soldiers fought as well as the whites, and some proved to be outstanding combat leaders. "No disciplinary or morale problems have arisen by reason of the integration of Negro soldiers into white units, and there has been no friction between the troops that could be traced to differences in color."

As against these reports of the advantageous results of integration came evidence of the deleterious effects of segregation. The record of the 24th Infantry Regiment has been spotty. Every company in the regiment, Martin relates, has fought magnificently at one time or another, but, on the other hand, every unit but one broke and ran at one time or another. "Officers of line companies, though, never knew whether their men would fight or run."

In situations where the soldier needs special confidence in his fellows, in his primary group—as in night attacks—the men in all-Negro units were particularly vulnerable. As one battalion commander said, "The trouble was, not one of them had any confidence that the other man would stay and fight, and each one had a terror of being left up there alone."

The feeling of security which the soldier ordinarily gets from the others of the primary group was here negated by the doubt in those others implanted by the larger society and manifested to him by the fact of segregation. As insightful an explanation of this as any, is found in Martin's quotation of the words of a Negro captain of a combat company.

"You put him in a white regiment, and he looks around him and sees white men and black men both, and he feels in his heart, 'now they are treating me like an American, not like a Negro.' But you put him in a Negro regiment, and he looks around him and sees nothing but Negroes, and he feels like somebody is using him as cannon fodder. He feels he is being treated not as an American soldier, but as a Negro soldier. And all the psychological inhibitions he has inherited through generations of living as a race apart—the lack of faith in himself, lack of confidence in his own race—take hold of him and he is hard to handle." (Martin, pp. 31, 140.)

The combat record of the all-Negro regiment and its morale improved after better-educated and more highly skilled replacements came in, and during the term of command of an unusually able officer who effected notable improvements before he was invalided out with ulcers. However, the disrupting influences of segregation apparently continued in this regiment as in other all-Negro units.

The most spectacular and widely publicized indication of such influences has been the unusual number of court-martial cases of men from all-Negro units for violating the 75th Article of War, misbehavior before the enemy. These cases were investigated by a Negro attorney, Thurgood Marshall, who visited Japan and Korea in the course of his inquiries. While he may not be an entirely impartial observer, his facts seem unassailable. He noted that only two white servicemen had been convicted of violating the

75th Article of War whereas 23 Negroes had been convicted on that charge. The majority of the court-martial cases of the Negroes, according to Thurgood Marshall, were the result of low morale induced by segregation. Marshall said he had studied integration in mixed groups and could find no evidence of large numbers of court-martial cases in any mixed unit. (*New York Times*, February 22, 1951, p. 4; March 2, 1951, p. 3; see also Weil, pp. 97–98.)

Whatever may have been the actuality in these trials, it is clear that in the Korean combat as elsewhere in the Army during war and peace, segregation foments complaints and causes the dissipation of energy in wasteful hostilities within the U.S. Army. That this is true of occupation troops as well as of combat troops is indicated in newspaper reports of May, 1951, which told of a café fight between white and Negro American soldiers in Karlsruhe, Germany, presumably because the white soldiers objected to the presence of Negro soldiers with German girls in the café. (*New York Times*, May 10, 1951, p. 14.)

By the middle of 1951, Army training programs and service schools were largely operated on a basis of racial integration, but the permanent unit to which a Negro soldier was assigned was still usually a segregated one. The former executive secretary of the Fahy Committee, noting that the Air Force and Navy had abolished segregation and that the Army had not yet done so, wrote early in 1951: "The Army, in short, has not lived up to the policy it announced just a year ago after months of negotiation with the President's Committee on Equality of Treatment and Opportunity." (Kenworthy, p. 27.)

One reason why the Army has moved more slowly in this respect is probably the fact that segregation has masked another Army problem, that of the utilization of men in class V, the lowest category of general-classification-test scores. The other services had heretofore been able to exclude such men by selective recruitment. The Army has had to take in large numbers of them. Under present practices of training and assignment, class-V men are not usually able to perform adequately in a modern army; for example, the combat efficiency of any kind of unit falls rapidly where over 10 per cent of the men are class V, according to the 1943 testimony of Major General I. H. Edwards. It may be that with training specially designed for their needs and if given tasks within their competence, class-V men would not be a drag on military efficiency. But such special training and assignment does not now exist.

Since the general-classification-test scores mainly reflect degree of education and other environmental advantages, a large proportion of all Negro recruits, whose education has been wanting and whose social environment has been disadvantaged, fall into class V. Thus the all-Negro Ninety-second Division in World War II went into battle with 50 per cent of its men in class V and 90 per cent in classes IV and V. (Kenworthy, p. 29.) So long as many class-V men could be lumped in segregated units, their deficiencies could be attributed to the racial factor and the problems of training and utilizing class-V men, of any color, passed over.

The relation of education to military performance is indicated by H. H. Martin's report of the 24th Infantry Regiment in Korea. He notes, as the former commander of the unit also does, that the unit's record improved when replacements came in who were better educated on the average than were the personnel when the regiment first fought in Korea. But this should not be interpreted to mean that better-educated Negro soldiers are less sensitive to the restrictions of segregation. It seems likely that they are all the more so, and the disadvantages of segregation will not be canceled in an all-Negro unit by assigning higher-scoring personnel to it.

Negro units have thus been doubly disadvantaged. All

the handicaps of the racial perspective, mentioned earlier in this survey, have hampered the performance of their higher-scoring men who could perform better in an integrated unit. And these units have tended to have a large proportion of class-V men who need special training to be adequate in any unit, segregated or integrated. The low-scoring men, also, may well do better in an integrated than in a segregated unit, but such improvement is still not sufficient. A class-V soldier, whether white or Negro, probably works more effectively in a smoothly coöperating unit than in a dispirited, disorganized one, but is not much of an asset even in the efficient unit.

A new development in Army policy became known on July 27, 1951, when it was announced that the 24th Infantry Regiment and all other Negro units in the Far East Command were to be disbanded. Both military and civilian considerations justify carrying out this procedure throughout the Army. But until better studies of human relations in the Army are made, until more basic social-science research is carried on, systematic guides for the implementation of such policy will not be available.[1]

Thus it appears from the evidence cited that the cohesive forces of the primary group in the Army tend to override racial prejudice; a Negro is generally accepted as a buddy by his white fellow soldiers. But there are probably certain conditions under which this does not necessarily operate. Moreover, the typical form and function of the primary group must be better formulated than is now possible. When better data on the primary group are available, when more is known of the variations in the influence of the primary group under different conditions, these policy decisions can be taken and implemented with a clearer notion than is now possible of the consequences which may be expected to follow the new development.

---

[1] A useful appraisal of research approaches and techniques which are pertinent to these problems has been made by R. M. Williams Jr., pp. 108–134.

Review /

There is not much scientific evidence bearing on the ways in which the men of a unit get themselves organized within the formal military organization, but there is a considerable amount of indirect evidence. The men who participate together in an informal organization make up the primary group.

The formal organization directs the activity and limits the range of behavior of the men so long as they operate as a military unit. But the men of the unit do not invariably operate according to the regulations and requirements of the formal organization; the informal organization is frequently a potent factor. This is clearly demonstrated in reviewing the effectiveness of unit leadership.

There is no doubt that competent leadership is usually necessary for militarily effective unit performance. And the qualities which a good officer-leader should have are a matter of general agreement. But there is a considerable difference between these ideal patterns and the actual behavior of many unit officers. This gap between the ideal—both of the published manuals and of the enlisted man's opinion—and the reality is frequently the result of a lack of identification between an officer and his men.

Some aspects of officer training make it difficult for the officer to establish this relationship. Without establishing identification an officer cannot readily be an effective leader; without effective officer-leaders a unit does not usually operate effectively. Identification between an officer and his men enhances his leadership largely because the officer can then have the support of the informal organization and of the primary-group standards of the men.

The importance of this organization and these standards is attested by many competent observers, most vividly in Marshall's study of infantry tactics. Colonel Marshall observes that American infantrymen in combat will usually fight only in the presence of men whom they know—in the presence of others of their primary group.

The primary group is so important because it is the only face-to-face group to which the soldier can belong, and he has an even stronger need to belong to such a group as a soldier than he did as a civilian. This group is of such great importance because of the cutting off of his previous social affiliations, because of the isolation from other groupings, because of the uniqueness of his experience within the unit, and because of the high degree of mutual dependence and responsibility in the primary group. Membership in a primary group helps the soldier by reducing his anxiety, by giving him a feeling that he counts as a person, and, in general, by enabling him to withstand the strains of army life which he might not otherwise be able to tolerate.

The primary group enforces certain standards in order to accomplish these group benefits. The soldier is not only the recipient of the group's benefits but also one of the donors of the benefits to others; he is subject to the group's mandates as well as being one of the administrators of its informal code. This code includes the adherence to norms of masculinity, the insistence on group solidarity, and the conferral of status other than that bestowed by external authority. These patterns are enforced by verbal taunts, by the withholding of privileges, and by ostracism. Newcomers are usually eager to join a primary group and quickly taken into one. The loyalty to the primary group is expressed as loyalty to the outfit.

In combat, all factors which make the primary group so important are intensified, and it becomes of crucial importance. The forces which actuate the soldier for long periods while he is in combat are significantly those which rise out of his primary-group affiliation.

The concept of the primary group and its dynamics may be used to set up a tentative explanation of the behavior of Negro units. A review of the historical evidence on the subject shows that integration has yielded results which are satisfactory from the standpoint of military performance, while segregation—in recent years at least—has been unsatisfactory by the same criterion.

Military commanders have tended to have needless misgivings about the use of Negro troops. When events forced such use, the prior apprehensions proved groundless. Thus General George Washington, on the advice of his staff and of a civilian committee, ordered that the Negroes, who were then in the Continental Army, were to be excluded from it, and further recruiting of Negroes was to be stopped. When this order was rescinded because of the threat of enemy propaganda to Negroes and for other reasons, Negroes continued to serve usefully and creditably in the Army. Union staff officers in the Civil War took two years to decide that Negroes should be used in the Union ranks. They gave a good account of themselves.

By the time of World War II, the question was not whether Negroes should serve in the armed forces, but how they were to be used. Despite staff studies which recommended either integration or small all-Negro units in white divisions, three all-Negro divisions were activated: mixed-company organization was not attempted because it was feared that such companies (of one Negro platoon in a company) would not work in combat. The three divisional groups were far from effective; when mixed companies were established because of great need for infantrymen, they worked very well.

The Navy excluded Negroes from general service for some years until it had to take them from Selective Service during World War II. Various military pressures led the Navy to experiment cautiously with integration. The experiments were so unconditionally successful that the Navy quickly abolished segregation and has now a policy of full integration.

When the Air Force established integrated units, base commanders feared trouble. No trouble ensued. On the contrary, there was less trouble caused by race differences than before.

Segregation in the modern army is not only unnecessarily inefficient in the use of manpower, and wasteful of materiel and facilities, but probably impairs the cohesion of the primary group when its members are under stress. While there have been and now are fine Negro units in the Army, the men of these units achieve efficiency *despite* the hindrances imposed by segregation. Segregation encourages a racial perspective so that the men tend to interpret everything unpleasant which happens to them in terms of racial discrimination. In segregated units, leadership tends to be less effective than in nonsegregated outfits, complaints tend to be more frequent and bitter, efficiency is frequently below the full potential, and morale—however morale may be measured—often ebbs low. This is true on the Army post whether in the United States or in Germany, and on the field of battle whether in Italy or in Korea.[1]

Combat increases the interdependence within the primary group, and the men of a segregated unit not infrequently flee from such life-and-death dependence on their fellows, a flight not taken by the same kind of men in an integrated unit. For segregation, our hypothesis states, is a continuous reminder to the men that a low opinion of their Negro fellows is held by parts of the larger society. And reject that valuation though many of them may, it undermines the confidence in each other which men of the primary group must have in order to face combat successfully. This is not the only reason for the relatively deficient combat performance of all-Negro units in recent years, but it was probably a factor of major importance.

Integration has worked well because under conditions of military service the forces which attract the soldier to and make him part of a primary group are powerful enough to override adverse racial attitudes. By the time the men of such a primary group enter combat the interpersonal bonds are firm enough to withstand the strain.

These effects of integration have occurred in all three armed services and under training, garrison, as well as combat conditions. White enlisted men do not strenuously resist integration nor do Negro enlisted men oppose it when integration is a matter of routine official procedure. But when soldiers, *before* they have experience with integration, are asked in a questionnaire whether they would like integration, the great majority of whites and a considerable proportion of Negroes express their opposition.

Once a Negro is placed in an integrated unit, however, he generally becomes part of the informal group—he acquires buddies. Among them his color makes little differ-

[1] A report on Negro troops in Korean combat which appeared in January 1952, bears out the earlier evidence. (Spore and Cocklin, 1952.)

ence, except where they defend him on that score against outsiders. Friction between individuals or groups, because of race, usually decreases when integration replaces segregation. This is so partly because the Negro's racial perspective, which sees discrimination at every hand, diminishes in an integrated unit; and partly because the white comrades of a Negro soldier are less likely to foment racial hostilities.

Further experience with or experiments in integration will indicate whether the cohesive influence of the primary group predominates in all possible situations. Thus integration may not have the same consequences as those heretofore recorded when instituted in a National Guard division from the deep South or in a unit which is predominantly Negro rather than predominantly white. And integration so far has been among enlisted men mainly. Few Negro Army officers have commanded integrated units. In the Air Force there are relatively few Negro officers and even fewer in the Navy. Experimental groups set up in the armed services and observed as part of a broad program of social-science research could contribute much to the advancement of both social-science theory and the applications of theory.

Bibliography /

AIR MINISTRY. GREAT BRITAIN
    1947. *Psychological Disorders in Flying Personnel of the Royal Air Force.* Air Publication 3139. London.

ANONYMOUS
    1946. "Informal Social Organization in the Army," *American Journal of Sociology,* vol. 51, pp. 365–370.
    1946. "The Making of the Infantryman," *American Journal of Sociology,* vol. 51, pp. 376–379.

ARDANT DU PICQ, C. J. J. J.
    1947. *Battle Studies.* The Military Service Publishing Company, Harrisburg.

BARNARD, C. I.
    1938. *The Functions of the Executive.* Harvard University Press, Cambridge.

BASSAN, MORTON E.
    1947. "Some Factors Found Valuable in Maintaining Morale on a Small Combatant Ship," *Bulletin of the Menninger Clinic,* vol. 25, pp. 33–42.

BERGER, MORROW
    1946. "Law and Custom in the Army," *Social Forces*, vol. 25, pp. 82–87.
BERKMAN, PAUL L.
    1946. "Life Aboard an Armed-Guard Ship," *American Journal of Sociology*, vol. 51, pp. 380–387.
BRADLEY, OMAR N.
    1951. *A Soldier's Story*. Holt, New York.
BROTZ, HOWARD, and EVERETT WILSON
    1946. "Characteristics of Military Society," *American Journal of Sociology*, vol. 51, pp. 371–375.
COHEN, R. A.
    1947. "Military Group Psychotherapy," *Mental Hygiene*, vol. 31, pp. 94–102.
COHEN, R. A., and J. G. DELANO
    1945. "Subacute Emotional Disturbances Induced by Combat," *War Medicine*, vol. 7, pp. 284–296.
COLEMAN, J. V.
    1946. "The Group Factor in Military Psychiatry," *American Journal of Orthopsychiatry*, vol. 16, pp. 222–225.
COON, C. S.
    1946. "The Universality of Natural Groupings in Human Societies," *The Journal of Educational Sociology*, vol. 20, pp. 163–168.
DAVENPORT, ROY K.
    1947. "The Negro in the Army: A Subject of Research," *Journal of Social Issues*, vol. 3, pp. 32–39.
DAVIS, A. K.
    1948. "Bureaucratic Patterns in the Navy Officer Corps," *Social Forces*, vol. 27, pp. 143–153.
DAVIS, KINGSLEY
    1949. *Human Society*. Macmillan, New York.
DEUTSCH, M.
    1949. "A Theory of Co-operation and Competition," *Human Relations*, vol. 2, pp. 129–152.
DOLLARD, CHARLES, and DONALD YOUNG
    1947. "In the Armed Forces," *Survey Graphic*, vol. 36, pp. 66–68, 111–116.

ELKIN, FREDERICK
1946. "The Soldier's Language," *American Journal of Sociology*, vol. 51, pp. 414–422.

FRANK, J. D.
1946. "Personal Problems Related to Army Rank," *American Journal of Psychiatry*, vol. 103, pp. 97–104.

GEORGE, COLLINS
1951. Articles in *Pittsburgh Courier*, April 7, 14, 21, 28, May 5, 12, 19, 26, June 2, 9, 16, 23, 30, July 7, 14, 21.

GRANGER, L. B.
1947. "Racial Democracy—The Navy Way," *Common Ground*, Winter Issue, pp. 61–68.

GRINKER, ROY R., and JOHN P. SPIEGEL
1945. *Men Under Stress*. Blakiston, Philadelphia.

GURVITCH, G., and W. E. MOORE
1945. *Twentieth Century Sociology*. Philosophical Library, New York.

HALL, E. T., JR.
1947. "Race Prejudice and Negro-White Relations in the Army," *American Journal of Sociology*, vol. 52, pp. 401–409.

HASTIE, W. H.
1943. *On Clipped Wings*. NAACP, Washington, D.C.

HOMANS, GEORGE C.
1946. "The Small Warship," *American Sociological Review*, vol. 11, pp. 294–300.
1950. *The Human Group*. Harcourt Brace, New York.

HUGHES, E. C.
1946. "The Knitting of Racial Groups in Industry," *American Sociological Review*, vol. 11, pp. 512–519.

JANIS, IRVING L.
1945. "Psychdynamic Adjustment to Army Life," *Psychiatry*, vol. 8, pp. 159–176.

JENKINS, WILLIAM O.
1947. "A Review of Leadership Studies with Particular Reference to Military Problems," *Psychological Bulletin*, vol. 44, pp. 54–79.

KENWORTHY, E. W.
1951. "The Case Against Army Segregation," *The Annals of the American Academy of Political and Social Science,* vol. 275, pp. 27–33.
KRECH, D., and R. S. CRUTCHFIELD
1948. *Theory and Problems of Social Psychology.* McGraw-Hill, New York.
MACIVER, R. M., and C. H. PAGE
1949. *Society.* Long and Smith, New York.
MARSHALL, S. L. A.
1947. *Men Against Fire,* Morrow, New York and Infantry Journal, Washington.
MARTIN, H. H.
1951. "How Do Our Negro Troops Measure Up?" *Saturday Evening Post,* June 16, pp. 30–31, 139–141.
MERTON, ROBERT K.
1949. *Social Theory and Social Structure.* The Free Press, Glencoe, Illinois.
MERTON, ROBERT K., and PAUL F. LAZARSFELD
1950. *Studies in the Scope and Method of "The American Soldier."* The Free Press, Glencoe, Illinois.
MYRDAL, G.
1944. *An American Dilemma.* Harper, New York.
NELSON, DENNIS D.
1948. *The Integration of the Negro into the United States Navy.* Navy Department, NAVEXOS-P-526, Washington, D.C.
NEWCOMB, T. M., and E. L. HARTLEY
1947. *Readings in Social Psychology.* Holt, New York.
O'GARA, H. P.
1945. "The GI's Morale," *Infantry Journal,* vol. 56, pp. 49–50.
PAGE, CHARLES H.
1946. "Bureaucracy's Other Face," *Social Forces,* vol. 25, pp. 88–94.
PIPPING, KNUT
1947. *Kompaniet Som Samhälle* (English summary entitled *The Social Life of a Machine Gun Company*). Acta Academiae Aboensis, Humaniora XVI, Åbo Akademi, Åbo, Finland.

PRATTIS, P. L.
  1943. "The Morals of the Negro in the Armed Services of the United States," *Journal of Negro Education*, vol. 12, pp. 355–363.
PRESIDENT'S COMMITTEE ON EQUALITY OF TREATMENT AND OP-PORTUNITY IN THE ARMED SERVICES
  1950. *Freedom to Serve*. Government Printing Office, Washington, D.C.
REDDICK, L. D.
  1947. "The Negro Policy of the United States Army, 1775–1945," *Journal of Negro History*, vol. 34, pp. 9–29.
ROSE, ARNOLD M.
  1945. "Bases of American Military Morale in World War II," *Public Opinion Quarterly*, vol. 9, pp. 411–417.
  1947. "Army Policies Toward Negro Soldiers: A Report on a Success and a Failure," *Journal of Social Issues*, vol. 3, pp. 26–31.
SCHNEIDER, D. M.
  1946. "The Culture of the Army Clerk," *Psychiatry*, vol. 9, pp. 123–129.
SPINDLER, G. D.
  1948. "The Military—A Systematic Analysis," *Social Forces*, vol. 27, pp. 83–88.
SPORE, J. B., and R. F. COCKLIN
  1952. "Our Negro Soldiers," *The Reporter*, vol. 6, pp. 6–9.
STAFFORD-CLARK, D.
  1949. "Morale and Flying Experience: Results of a War-Time Study," *Journal of Mental Science*, vol. 95, pp. 10–50.
STOUFFER, S. A., *et al.*
  1949. *The American Soldier*. Vol. i: *Adjustment During Army Life;* vol. ii: *Combat and Its Aftermath*. Princeton University Press, Princeton.
STONE, R. C.
  1946. "Status and Leadership in a Combat Fighter Squadron," *American Journal of Sociology*, vol. 51, pp. 388–394.
U.S. WAR DEPARTMENT
  1947. "Negro Manpower in the Army," *Army Talk No. 170*. Washington, D.C.

WEIL, F. E. G.
  1947. "The Negro in the Armed Forces," *Social Forces,* vol. 26, pp. 95–98.
WHITE, H. B.
  1946. "Military Morality," *Social Research,* vol. 13, pp. 410–440.
WILLIAMS, R. M., JR.
  1947. *The Reduction of Intergroup Tensions.* Social Science Research Council, Bulletin 57, New York.
WILLIAMS, S. B., and H. J. LEAVITT
  1947. "Methods of Selecting Marine Corps Officer Candidates," in G. A. Kelley, ed., *New Methods in Applied Psychology.* University of Maryland, College Park (Md.)
WILSON, L., and W. L. KOLB
  1949. *Sociological Analysis.* Harcourt Brace, New York.

Index /

of, in combat, 89–90, 122–124; in World War II army, 93–106, 130; military disadvantages of, 90, 94–96, 99–101; modification of, in Army, 102–104; primary group in relation to, 18, 92–93, 122–123

Shils, E. A., 30–31, 44, 57, 60–61, 72–74, 76

Smith, M. B., 14, 17, 32, 58, 59, 62, 74–75

Social organization of Army: hierarchy of, 11–14; results on informal grouping, 12–15; role of unit officer in, 15–16

Speier, Hans, 48, 62–63

Spiegel, John P., 8, 18, 21, 78, 80–81, 84

Spindler, G. D., 45

Spore, J. B., 131

Stafford-Clark, D., 81, 84

Stone, R. C., 51, 52, 66, 71

Stouffer, S. A., 6–7, 10, 14, 16–17, 19, 23, 24, 25–26, 29, 31, 32, 33, 34, 44, 47, 48, 58, 60, 62, 63, 65, 66, 67, 68, 74–75, 77, 80, 82, 83, 84, 85, 94, 95, 96, 102, 104, 107

Suchman, E. A., 47, 60

Symonds, Sir Charles P., 21–22

Tests: aptitude, 19–20; general classification, 20, 101, 124–125, 126; mechanical aptitude, 20; psychological, 9, 10

Thirty-first Division, 118

Twenty-fifth [XXV] Corps, 91

Twenty-fourth Infantry Regiment, 122, 125, 126

Union Army, 91

Washington, General George, 91, 94, 129

Wavell, Field Marshal Sir Archibald, 86

Weil, F. E. G., 124

White, H. B., 30, 75

Williams, D. J., 21–22

Williams, R. M., Jr., 14, 32, 126

Williams, S. B., 20

Wilson, Everett, 51, 53

Wilson, L., 39, 65

Young, Donald, 99–101, 103

www.ingramcontent.com/pod-product-compliance
Lightning Source LLC
Chambersburg PA
CBHW031138270326
41929CB00011B/1669